Heart Essence

Also by Rob Preece

Heart Essence

Enhancing Qualities of the Awakening Mind

Rob Preece

Mudra Publications
Devon, 2022

Mudra Publications
1 Church Park Cottages
Holne
Devon TQ13 7SG
UK.

www.mudra.co.uk

ISBN: 978-1-7399402-1-8

Edited by Diane Schaap

Cover design by Rob Preece

Contents

The Essence of Tantra Series

Tantric practice is a profound approach to the complete transformation and liberation of our body, speech and mind from what limits and obscures their natural potential. Often, the visualisation of colourful and inspiring deities is considered central to this way of practice. This is partly true – but tantric practice is so much more when we fully understand how it 'works'. Tantra becomes a way of integrating many different aspects of our life into a radical process of awakening. Our mind, our emotional and psychological life, our creative life, our body and relationships are all aspects of this process. All that we are is included within this path of alchemical transformation.

In this *Essence of Tantra Series* of books, following on from *Tasting the Essence of Tantra*, I will be looking at particular aspects of tantric practice in more detail. Much of the material included in these books has grown out of the four-year *Tasting the Essence of Tantra* series of modules I taught in Europe, the US and the UK over the past twelve years. These modules gave me the opportunity to gather together the essential ingredients of tantric practice and explore how effective they are in relation to our contemporary life and psychological nature. It also provided the opportunity to explore a way of practice that was much more deeply rooted in the body and the process of meditation rather than being oriented towards the recitation of *sadhana* texts.

The word *tantra* in Sanskrit is often translated as 'weave'. When we go more deeply into the nature of tantric practice, we discover a weave or matrix of ways of transformation and healing that are profound and, in many ways, radical. In this series of books, I will explore an approach to personal transformation that has particular significance for our contemporary psychological life. The practices I will introduce represent a healing matrix that can address some of the key psychological challenges many of us can experience in our lives. These are practices that can also enable us to awaken qualities that are at the heart of a bodhisattva's capacity to manifest in the world whatever is beneficial for the welfare of others.

Some books in this series will focus on specific deity practices; others will explore significant aspects of tantra such as the nature of the mandala and the cultivation of bodhicitta, the awakening heart essence, as it relates to tantric practice. During this process I will also introduce certain meditations which are intended to demonstrate the creative nature of tantric practice. This is a reflection of how I was taught by my primary teacher Lama Thubten Yeshe, who saw that tantra could be explored in a creative way. Much of what I draw upon here comes from the richness of experience this more creative approach can bring and how it can specifically address our psychological disposition as Westerners. I have been involved in these practices for almost 50 years and have spent a great deal of time in retreat teaching and guiding others. Through that experience I have discovered many ways in which tantric practice can transform and awaken our inner reality. It can be an extraordinary gift and presence in our life. In each of these books I will remain true to the essence of the tantric path, and I wish to bring to that path a freshness in how we can integrate it in our lives. What primarily interests me is how we each can experience tantra as a living inner process, not just the technicalities of a system of practices. This series of books gives me the opportunity to explore this extraordinary path through two lenses: the profound richness of the Tibetan tradition as well as invaluable insights that come from my Jungian psychology background. My hope is that the confluence of these perspectives will enrich and inspire your journey as it has my own.

Dedication

I dedicate Heart Essence to all those I have worked with over the years in the context of psychotherapy, mentoring and teaching. I offer my deep appreciation and gratitude for the trust they placed in me by allowing me to travel alongside them on their journey. I have learned so much from their openness and honesty as well as from the pain and struggle some have been through and the wonderful revelations and insights that have also emerged in that process. So much of what I write has been inspired by this work.

I also offer my gratitude to Anna for her supportive presence in this work and to Diane Schaap for helping this book come into form.

May the blessings of the buddhas always be with you and support you in your journey.

Thank you.

Introduction

A T THE HEART OF BUDDHISM is the wish for all beings to be free of suffering. This grows out of the recognition, taught by the Buddha in the *first noble truth*, that life is pervaded by suffering. This wish is taken to a deeper level by the *bodhisattva*, who dedicates this and future lives to be of greatest benefit to sentient beings by actively liberating them from suffering. Undaunted by the extent of their suffering, the bodhisattva cultivates the courage and commitment to remain engaged in the world, despite its challenges and turmoil, to serve others. This engagement is supported by a growing capacity to awaken and to embody qualities of love, compassion, courage and wisdom that are attributes of our pristine buddha-nature. The combination of intense and consuming compassion for the chronic suffering of others with an understanding of our extraordinary human potential to awaken is a powerful cocktail. It can generate a compelling intention that sees awakening to our innate buddha potential as the most beneficial way to liberate others from suffering and bring the greatest sense of meaning to this life. This intention, known as bodhicitta, or the "awakening mind", is not based in our ordinary conceptual mind; it is the awakening of a deeper quality of heart mind or *heart essence*.

The bodhisattva as the "awakening warrior" is willing to endure the hardships of the path of awakening and to remain in the world to serve others rather than attain a state of liberation that eventually becomes divorced from embodied existence. In Buddhism as it evolved in India after the time of the Buddha, two distinct paths began to emerge. One path sought self-liberation, a state that no longer needed to be reborn in the cycle of existence. A second path, the *Mahayana*, or "greater vehicle", considered this liberation as not serving the welfare of others in a way that is possible by remaining in embodied form and continuing to live in the world. The bodhisattva chooses this second path.

This courageous path requires a bodhisattva to engage with life fully and with an openness of the heart that does not run away from the trials and challenges life brings. The power of bodhicitta makes this possible. Shantideva, the 11th-century Indian scholar, says in his *Guide to the Bodhisattva's Way of Life* that when bodhicitta is born it is "like a flash of lightning on a dark night that illuminates everything". [1] He saw bodhicitta as an extraordinary disposition that, once awakened, will bring illumination to countless others in their darkness. He saw it as the "universal medicine" that would cure all ills, and as an elixir that transforms our ordinary nature into the quality of a buddha. He considered bodhicitta to be a quality of heart that would overcome all the evils in the world. Shantideva also made it very clear that, while there are many different aspects to the Buddhist path, it is only bodhicitta that gives rise to the fully awakened nature of a buddha. Within the Tibetan tradition are many inspiring, complicated deity practices and different forms of yogic energy exercises – but without bodhicitta these do not lead to buddhahood.

H.H. Dalai Lama describes the nature of bodhicitta as an attitude of "universal responsibility"[2] that sees caring for the welfare of others as paramount. This is a disposition we sorely need in the world today when there is so much self-interest at the expense of others. Although the suffering that we seem capable of inflicting upon each other can appear to be endless, we are all capable of awakening this heart of bodhicitta. We all have this potential within our nature, but we are often unable to overcome those emotional habits and wounds that prevent it from manifesting.

We all have the capacity for love and kindness, but its expression will be limited until we open our hearts. Our potential for compassion and empathy emerges when we allow the suffering of others to touch us. Equally, it is possible for the attitude of bodhicitta to grow if we know how to enable this to happen. Within the Tibetan tradition are various approaches to meditation that help this cultivation of bodhicitta. These I have described in my book *The Courage to Feel*. What I want to explore here are the different facets of bodhicitta as it emerges and how we can understand the psychological implications of this emergence.

I see bodhicitta as a multifaceted jewel where many different qualities come together to make up the whole. Chenrezig, the buddha of compassion, is sometimes described as the jewel within the lotus; his mantra OM MANI PADME HUNG means exactly this. This is the heart jewel of bodhicitta. Figure 1 shows the facets of that jewel which make up the quality of bodhicitta. Each of these facets has gradually become clearer to me through my own exploration of this path, learning explicitly from many of my guides and also seeing how they expressed and embodied the qualities of bodhicitta. To cultivate these facets often requires that we begin to heal areas of our psychological nature that may obstruct their natural expression. As we begin to explore them we may see where we need further investigation of our own difficulties in order to grow. We may also recognise those facets of our emerging bodhicitta that already feel natural and awake and that simply need to be brought more fully into awareness. Together these different ingredients make up a whole that is much greater than the sum of the parts. Bodhicitta is a heartfelt quality, not just the thought "I must get enlightened for the sake of sentient beings". Like a powerful river that runs through us, it is a profound feeling that moves us in our life and will inform all that we do from the depth of our being.

At this time in history the example of the bodhisattva is needed perhaps more than ever. As we begin to cultivate the qualities contained within the nature of bodhicitta, they can give us the courage and openness to live in a turbulent world full of great pain, fear, insecurity and anger. To be able to remain clear and present to the suffering of others, without being overwhelmed, requires that we develop the inner resourcefulness that bodhicitta can bring. If you are drawn to the path of the bodhisattva, then what I am exploring here will, I hope, help to awaken those inner capacities that can make this journey more steady and clear.

I am including this book in the *Essence of Tantra Series* because I want to bring the understanding of bodhicitta into the particular context of tantric practice. This quality of heart is the underlying intention that flavours how we embark upon tantric practice; equally, tantric practice flavours the way in which we can embody this desire to be of benefit to others. The *tantric bodhisattva*, as a vehicle for our buddha potential to manifest in the world, brings a particular potency to the quality of bodhicitta. Within tantric practice, our relationship to a deity enhances the way in which we begin to embody and manifest aspects of our innate buddha-nature in our life. A deity such as Chenrezig, often seen as the bodhisattva of compassion, is an expression or vision of our innate wholeness that deeply informs the nature of bodhicitta. Here I wish to explore ways in which awakening the *heart essence* of bodhicitta within the context of tantric understanding and practice has profound implications for how we can embody the bodhisattva's way of life.

Figure 1
The Jewel of Bodhicitta

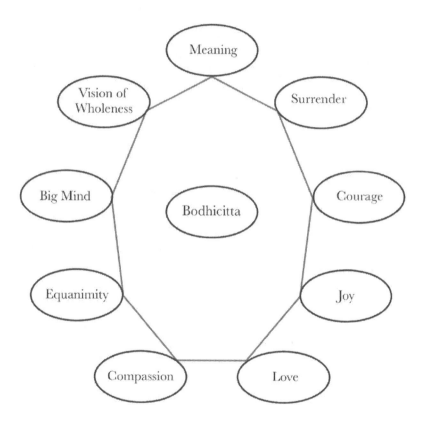

Figure 2
Chenrezig, the Buddha of Compassion

1

Compassion

I WISH TO BEGIN this exploration of the jewel of bodhicitta by considering perhaps the most significant quality of a bodhisattva, namely compassion. Compassion is one of the four *brahmaviharas*, which are often called the *four immeasurables* or *four infinite minds* (Sanskrit: *apramana*), and it is central to Buddhist life in all traditions. Together, the four brahmaviharas – compassion, love, joy and equanimity – could be seen as the ground or base from which bodhicitta emerges.

Compassion is an extraordinary attribute in our human nature that can arise spontaneously when we allow the suffering of another to touch us. The Tibetans often define compassion as the very basic wish that others may be free of suffering. This in turn can be expressed in the intention to actively liberate others from suffering in whatever way is most appropriate. When we are touched by the suffering of another, our compassion will often naturally motivate us to do something to alleviate their distress. We can see how this generates much of our human endeavour to seek ways to alleviate the suffering of others, whether in response to sickness, poverty, social upheaval or natural disasters. Thankfully we have this strong collective desire to engage with the suffering of others who live with us on the planet.

If we have suffered in some way that closes us off from our feelings, however, this natural capacity may not be so accessible to us. The presence of compassion is fundamental to our human health, and if we have not experienced it while growing up, we can be left emotionally disadvantaged. If we have experienced trauma in our relationship to others, the damage this may have caused can limit our capacity for compassion. Many of us are able to feel compassion towards another's suffering but not always feel it towards ourselves. Some people feel intense compassion for the suffering of an animal but are more challenged to feel this for humans. If we are to truly develop the capacity to open our compassionate nature to embrace the suffering of others, we may first need to heal our own inner wounding. In my own journey, I became aware of the degree to which I felt unable to be compassionate towards myself. I had a painfully harsh and critical inner landscape that was unforgiving in how I related to my flaws and vulnerabilities. As a therapist I have seen this time and again in clients who have suffered a critical or abusive parent or an early life that lacked a compassionate presence.

If we experience a lack of self-compassion, it is necessary to begin to heal this wound by developing an inner quality of acceptance and kindness that allows us to be as we are. We all have our qualities and our struggles; that is part of being human. Rather than judging or making ourselves wrong or bad, we need a sense of acceptance and compassion. If we can begin to grow this inner atmosphere, we will increasingly be able to hold that same disposition towards others with greater ease. Something that can help in this process is coming into relationship with someone who shows compassion towards us. If we can genuinely receive that compassion, it can then begin to shift our inner reality. The two contexts that I felt particularly aided the healing of my own lack of self-compassion were in relation to my Tibetan teacher Lama Yeshe and in the holding presence of some of the psychotherapists I have worked with over the years. I am thankful that in my own therapy I experienced a compassionate environment that truly allowed me to begin to heal and accept myself as I am. This was an enormous help in enabling me to feel a greater sense of compassion for others.

Once we have begun to heal our own inner relationship to self-compassion, the outward expression of compassion towards others may manifest in a number of ways. While compassion can often be very active, another important quality, *compassionate presence*, is less to do with alleviating someone's pain or suffering directly and immediately and more with simply holding someone in their distress. It is this latter aspect of compassion that I want to particularly emphasise here, something I found was essential in my work as a psychotherapist – and not always easily learned. When we have a strong tendency to want to make things better, compassionate presence requires something different.

For me the deity Chenrezig (Figure 2) particularly embodies compassionate presence. His name in Tibetan means "he who looks upon all beings with the eyes of compassion." He embodies a profound sense of being with our pain in a way that truly witnesses it and holds it with compassionate awareness. His grounded form shows us how we can embody a capacity to allow someone's suffering to touch us without always having to act. Can we let ourselves be touched by someone's pain and allow them to be with their experience rather than taking it from them to make it all right? Often the question is: all right for whom? If I find someone's suffering unbearable then I want to make it better but, as I found in my experience as a therapist, this is not always what is needed. "Making it better" is not always the best way for a process of healing to unfold. When I am struggling I do not usually want someone to take my pain away. What has been more helpful is having someone present who truly hears my distress and can be with it in a caring and holding way. Then something begins to change.

We see that compassion is not straightforward. It is not only the wish that someone might be free of suffering that moves us to act; it can also be the growing capacity to bear another's pain and suffering and be present with them as they go through it. Compassionate presence is perhaps the greatest gift we can give to another. It is what we needed as a child but didn't always receive. When we do receive it, we can be as we are without fear of judgement. I feel this is the gift of Chenrezig: a quality of compassion that is unconditional and free of judgement.

Another aspect of compassionate presence that I feel Chenrezig embodies is steadiness. His posture always gives me the sense of not being shaken by our suffering. He does not go into an urgency of having to sort it out. He is not thrown off balance by our pain; he can bear it. (For an in-depth exploration of the healing nature of the practice of Chenrezig, I recommend *Chenrezig, Embodying Compassionate Presence* in the *Essence of Tantra Series*.) This has been an important capacity for me as a therapist when clients have needed to tell the most horrendous stories that could easily feel overwhelming if I was deeply attuned through empathy. Empathy, as a sensitivity to resonate with someone's pain, is an important capacity alongside compassion. But empathy can become too sensitive and then we can easily become overwhelmed. By contrast, compassion has an objectivity to it that helps us find an appropriate proximity to someone's pain without becoming lost in it. This allows a certain level of steadiness that can enable us to hear someone's terrible experience and yet stay present and hold a space that is caring and not judging.

When we are close to another, a natural inner mechanism brings us into a resonance with their state of being. This resonance can have a very positive effect, and a parent can often provide this when their child is in distress. When the parent can stay relatively peaceful and compassionate, undisturbed yet steady and present, this has a natural effect on the child. It provides a sense of safety that enables the child's nervous system to begin to settle and come into a quieter place. Likewise, in the therapeutic context I have felt that if I can remain in a relatively peaceful and undisturbed state while a client goes through their distress, this has a calming effect upon their nervous system. Compassionate presence affects those we support through this resonance. They pick up a sense that they are all right on some deep level and can go through their pain.

I am focusing upon compassionate presence here because I feel it is often not emphasised when we are viewing compassion as the wish to free others from suffering. There is and always will be the need to act and respond to the suffering around us. But this active capacity is also something that we need to learn how to express skilfully so that our actions to help another are truly based in the wisdom that sees what is genuinely needed. Perhaps this wisdom comes in part by listening to what the other tells us they need, rather than by assuming we know. All too often, when I was a social worker many years ago, I could see us assuming we knew what was good for someone. Sadly, this was often not the case.

Compassionate presence as I have been describing it is naturally focused on a specific relationship to another. In addition to this focused compassion, there is another aspect which is the extraordinary potential for an open and spacious quality that pervades our environment like the moisture in the atmosphere. I have felt these two contrasting aspects of compassionate presence, focused and spacious, when in the presence of H.H. Dalai Lama, who perhaps is the most famous embodiment of Chenrezig. Sitting amongst a large group of people when he is teaching, there is an almost tangible atmosphere of his compassionate quality. It is like moisture that pervades the space and gives a deep sense of ease and safety, so that all seems well in the world. Then, when he shifted this spacious attention to focus upon a visiting Tibetan who had just come from Tibet, his compassion seemed to become completely absorbed in that one person as though they were the only important one in the world for that moment in time. His compassion became focused on a specific relationship like a condensed drop of water. When the person went away I could feel that His Holiness opened his awareness again and returned to that pervasive sense of compassionate holding.

As in the example of His Holiness, compassion can focus upon someone specifically or it can be vast and open without reference to a particular relationship. We can consider the notion of boundless or *immeasurable compassion* in two possible ways. The first of these refers to the compassion that is open to every living creature without exception, whether they are a tiny ant or a rich celebrity. Every being is viewed with the same open heart of compassion because they all wish to experience happiness and yet, out of ignorance, often create the causes for suffering. The second way to understand this boundless nature comes from our experience of the nature of the mind and relates to the Sanskrit term *apramana,* or infinite mind. When we go beyond our narrow, contracted, ordinary mind and its view of reality, we can open to the spacious awareness that is the mind's ultimate nature. Within this totally open spacious awareness, the quality of compassion is like moisture pervading space. When, through meditation, we open to our *big mind* as I will describe it in Chapter 6, our compassion can become boundless in the way I have described the feeling of the Dalai Lama's presence.

Our compassion can become all-embracing. When it is, we meet the world with an openness and care that is free of judgements, prescriptions and agendas. When it becomes focused upon an individual, it is a natural presence that can be a wonderful healing gift. Compassion is at the root of the emergence of bodhicitta and grows through experience. Compassion can be like a muscle that grows in capacity the more we allow ourselves to exercise it. Today, however, as the news media constantly assails us with reports of the terrible suffering occurring in people's lives around the world, sometimes we may feel overwhelmed and unable to cope with its continual impact. When this happens, we may need to limit what we take in. When our experience of the suffering of others becomes too painful and overwhelming, we can potentially become drawn into an emotionally depressed place that is hard to bear. We may have too much sensitivity and empathy so that our capacity for compassion becomes overwhelmed with emotional distress. But Lama Yeshe used to say that "compassion is not sentimentality", meaning that it is not emotional. The great Tibetan dzogchen master Longchenpa[3] had a very interesting perspective on this. He considered that when one of the four brahmaviharas became emotionally disturbed, one of the other three would be a natural remedy. In the case of compassion, he felt that when it veered towards a more negative helpless or depressive place, the inclusion of joy would help reaffirm a positive, hopeful sense of what is possible and what can be transformed (see Figure 3). If we can open to the quality of joy, we will not fall into a place of hopelessness, helplessness or despair but instead regain a sense of optimism and hope.

As we gradually grow in our capacity to let more of the suffering in the world touch us, that suffering can support and strengthen our compassion. That compassion can then support and strengthen our desire to be of benefit to others, either in an active way or through compassionate presence. The natural transition for this deepening and expanding sense of compassion is that it evolves into bodhicitta. Bodhicitta enables us to bear the immensity of suffering we see around us because it leads us to recognise that we can awaken a potential within, our buddha-nature, that can be of greatest benefit to liberate others from that suffering.

The four brahmaviharas or *four immeasurable thoughts* are considered immeasurable because they are limitless in their scope towards all sentient beings. A verse familiar to Tibetan Buddhists expresses this quality in relationship to compassion:

How wonderful it would be if all beings were free from
suffering and the causes of suffering.
May they be free of suffering and its cause,
May I free them from suffering and its cause,
Bless me all you buddhas to be able to do this.

If we meditate upon this verse we can feel an evolution in its meaning. We begin with the wish that all beings without exception may be free of suffering and its cause. This wish evolves in the second line with the thought "May they be free", and still further with the third line where the clear intention is to take personal responsibility to free them. This brings us into relationship with the quality of bodhicitta, where we open to receive the blessings of the buddhas to fulfil this intention.

Figure 3
The Dynamic of the Four Immeasurables
(Longchenpa)

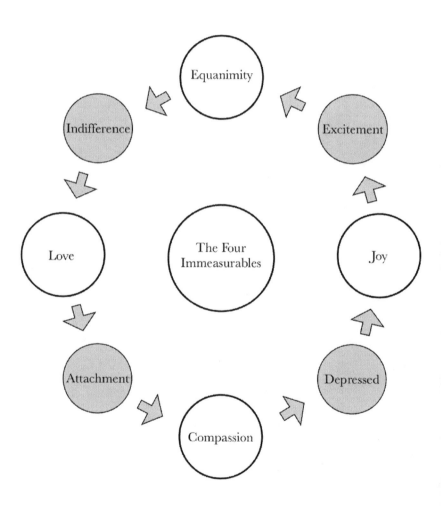

2

Love

THIS NEXT QUALITY I have intentionally called simply "love" rather than the term "loving kindness" that is often used in the Buddhist world. I am not so comfortable with this latter term because I feel it dilutes the full potency of love, becoming rather a quality that predicates kindness – that is to say kindness that is loving. What I wish to feel is the fullness of love, and from that love a natural kindness will manifest.

As I begin to reflect upon the nature of love in the context of bodhicitta, I find myself struggling for language to describe the subtleties and nuances of a feeling of the heart. From one perspective, one could see all four of the brahmaviharas as different aspects of the nature of love, where love brings us into a close and caring relationship to another. But love can be experienced and expressed in many different ways, from the love of a parent towards a child to the feeling of being "in love". Many Christians have a particularly strong sense of the significance of love in their relationship to God as the presence or pervasion of love at the heart of our reality. This gives me a similar feeling to the pervasive nature of compassion I have spoken of in the previous chapter. When our mind is totally opened to its innate spaciousness, clarity and awareness, boundless love will be a natural outflow. I felt this wonderful quality of love emanating from my primary teacher, Lama Thubten Yeshe. His love also pervaded the space while he was teaching us as we sat together in a large group. His warmth and quality of heart would give such a sense of well-being and joy that we bathed in it as in warm sunlight. When I would go and see him privately, this pervasive sense of his love would become focused and directly relational. This expression of his love then felt much more direct and personal and was an extraordinary quality of presence. I would go to see him with all manner of questions and concerns I wanted to ask about, but as soon as I was in his presence they seemed to melt away. I just felt that all was fine in the world and I was deeply loved.

Lama Yeshe's love had the feel of something that emanated from the heart, a sense of warmth that cherished others because he held them dear in the heart. Ironically, he also suffered from a heart disorder that would actually make his physical heart swell up in his chest. As he came closer to the end of his life this heart problem clearly troubled him, not so much for his own sake, but because he wanted to give so much to his students. I feel a deep sense of gratitude for the way Lama Yeshe gave himself, out of love, to those of us who were his students. His generosity of heart was a powerful expression of his extraordinary love. Lama's presence enabled my entry into the Tibetan tradition to be held by his wonderful capacity of joy, kindness and encouragement.

As I became involved in the Tibetan teachings on the cultivation of bodhicitta, however, I found something they spoke about very difficult to hear. They would repeatedly use the phrase that all suffering arose from the "self-cherishing mind". It was seen as the greatest of evils, a view I found incredibly distressing, though at first I did not understand why. What I was able to see was that it made me feel terrible about myself in a very unhelpful way. I began to realise that it was so disturbing because I really didn't cherish myself; in fact, I mostly felt a sense of something close to self-loathing. I could see that for me to begin to cultivate bodhicitta I needed to change this inner reality. I actually needed to begin to cherish myself in a healthy, loving way. But cultivating self-love felt like an extraordinarily difficult thing to do, and this was made even more difficult by the message that self-cherishing was a root of all harm and suffering. How was I to deal with this contradiction?

Any of us who suffer in this way must first take seriously the need to heal our inner wounds around our lack of self-love and self-value before the qualities of bodhicitta can freely emerge. Because these feelings almost always originate from early in our life, that is where the healing needs to begin. The idea of our inner child may, to some, seem like a psychological cliché, but it is a useful place to start when considering the process of healing. Many of us retain from our very young childhood a lack of self-value, a sense that we are not good enough or even that we are not lovable. If we can begin to recognise these wounds within our lack of self-love, we can use this in a healing process. For me one of the practices that has helped greatly is *tonglen*. I have included this practice at the end of this book and would highly recommend using it. In the process of healing our inner child, we can begin by visualising ourselves as a child in the space in front. This child may be at whatever age we feel the wound is most present. With the child there before us, we tune into how they were and to the painful sense of the lack of love and self-value. As with the usual tonglen practice we then consider taking away that suffering as we breathe in and then breathing out a sense of love and appreciation. If we practice in this way it can begin to have the effect of healing our inner relationship to our sense of self. It will often restore a feeling of connectedness to ourselves and to our life stream as we grew from childhood into being an adult. From this healthier place we can then more readily open to others while coming from a feeling of our own love and value.

In my own experience, this growing sense of self-love and self-value changed my inner preoccupation and enabled me to turn outwards towards others with greater appreciation and love. This gradual shift also made me realise that the problem is not one of self-cherishing; it is more the painful self-preoccupation and narcissism that persists so long as we feel emotionally wounded. As we heal this wound to our sense of self, our capacity to open to and cherish others can begin from a place of health.

I have sometimes felt my own capacity for love was more of a challenge than my capacity for compassion. As I grew up, my experience of love from my mother was always loaded with a level of anxiety and need that often felt too much to bear. I felt myself closing off to it in order to protect myself. As I began to have intimate relationships, I could also see that my love could easily be full of romantic fantasies and longings that would often lead to very painful experiences. To protect myself from hurt, again I learned to close my heart. In my exploration of Jung, I began to see the difference between being "in love", with all of its romantic projections and longings, and the deeper sense of love towards a person as they are. The "in love" state did not feel particularly real because there was a feeling of being beguiled by my projections, whereas to feel genuine love for someone has always felt very immediate and present.

When I began to work as a therapist I felt my capacity for love was held back because of my concern about how it would be received. I feared that, as a man, feeling love for my clients, particularly women, could be easily misunderstood. I was very aware of the dangers of therapists falling in love with clients and then abusing the relationship for their own desires. As a result, I found myself holding back until I gradually began to trust that I knew how to love without needing anything from my clients. When I eventually began to allow myself to open my heart to clients as I worked with them, it had a very dramatic effect on how I held them in the therapeutic relationship. I had the sense that they also felt that my love nourished and touched them deeply. It made me very aware that love needed to also be held within a sense of safety, without seeking to gain or receive something in return. Part of the wounding of some of my younger female clients was that they had experienced a father whose love was full of underlying agendas that were often of a sexual nature. For all clients, but especially for clients like these, I had to be sure that my love was safe and unconditional.

Love can bring closeness, trust and a sense of safety when it is expressed freely and without expectation. Love is a quality of presence, and loving kindness is an active ingredient that naturally emerges from it. Kindness, care and consideration become a natural outflow when love is present because we are sensitive to the needs and concerns of the other. The Tibetans describe love as the wish that others may be endowed with happiness. This phrase conveys that the warmth, care and concern within love is given off or emanated in the valuing and appreciation of another. Love brings us into closer proximity as we move towards another to cherish them with our warmth and kindness. What makes this safe and trustworthy is not only that the love can be unconditional, without the need for something in return, but also that we are able to remain present and separate. My experience of my mother was that this was not easy for her. Because she needed something from me, her love felt sticky and merging. Consequently, when I began to work with my clients I knew that any subtle need expressed within my love could be felt as a stickiness that was not helpful. Love allows another the freedom to be themselves and not necessarily as we want them to be. Can I love someone as they are, freely and openly? This is not usually the disposition of being "in love" with its many projections and expectations.

Once again I want to refer here to something Longchenpa considered in relation to the four immeasurable thoughts when they become emotionally disturbed. He believed that when love becomes too emotionally attached there can be a kind of smothering that needs to be remedied. When this happens there can be an outflow of feeling that loses the sense of separation and objectivity, bringing a tendency to merge. If this arises, Longchenpa said, we need to bring back the objectivity of compassion that recognises the other and their nature as a separate sentient being with their own reality and their own potential for suffering (see Figure 3). This implies that love also needs to retain a sense of the other as a separate being while maintaining a deep sense of connection.

As I have suggested, love can have a sense of focus that responds to and cares for an individual with warmth and kindness. Love also has the vast and open quality that is similar to compassion. This can be a love that embraces and values all life and holds it with totally open, unconditional care. It can also be an expression of the open spacious nature of mind when we shift from our relatively limited dualistic mind. In the practice of mahamudra we begin to make this shift away from the ordinary conceptual mind to a quality of open and spacious awareness. This *big mind,* which I will refer to later, can become pervaded by the totally open nature of immeasurable love in a way that can feel almost ecstatic.

The verse that the Tibetans often express in relation to the brahmavihara of immeasurable love is oriented to an awareness of a quality of love that recognises the suffering of limitless sentient beings and wishes them to experience happiness:

> *How wonderful it would be if all beings were endowed with*
> *happiness and the causes of happiness.*
> *May they be endowed with happiness and its cause,*
> *May I endow them with happiness and its cause,*
> *Bless me all you buddhas to be able to do this.*

As with the verse associated with limitless compassion, we see a gradual evolution. We begin with a simple wish that all beings without exception may be happy. This moves towards an aspiration in the second line and then an actual engagement in the third line. The thought "May I endow them with happiness" is a movement towards bodhicitta when combined with the request to the buddhas to enable us to awaken to be able to do this.

The two verses, of limitless compassion and love, are very powerful to combine in the practice of *tonglen*. We reflect upon the first verse, with compassion, and as we breathe in we open to take on others' suffering. With the second verse, on the out-breath, we emanate happiness and its cause. (Please see the Appendix for a more detailed explanation of this meditation.)

3

Joy

M<small>ANY</small> YEARS AGO Lama Zopa Rinpoche suggested to me that it would be good to practice rejoicing. I was intrigued by this; I wondered if he knew I had a mildly depressive nature and would sometimes become stuck in a pessimistic feeling about life. I was reminded that, if I really look at how my life is, I can see how fortunate I have been. I also recognised that if I can retain the sense of gratitude, I am more able to also rejoice in the fortune of others. It is said in many Tibetan teachings that the highest practice is to rejoice in the virtues of others. If we do so, our own virtuous mind will increase and the merit generated will benefit both ourselves and others. Our capacity to rejoice in and appreciate another's qualities and gifts in a totally open way is a significant aspect of the brahmavihara of joy.

The third brahmavihara is sometimes called *sympathetic joy*, which has interesting implications in our relationships to others. "Sympathetic" has several meanings. One of these is associated with qualities like the capacity to be responsive, receptive, sensitive and resonant. These associations all suggest a sensitivity and resonance between oneself and another, an ability to appreciate how the other feels and to respond in a positive way. Another meaning is associated with the capacity to be comforting, supportive and considerate from a place of care and appreciation. Both of these senses of the word require that we have some inner resource that enables us to naturally experience sympathetic joy; without this resource it can be a challenge. All of this leads me to consider that there are two dimensions to joy, one that is purely an inner feeling of well-being and the other that is a response in relationship to another person. If we do not have the former it is not easy to feel the latter.

If we do not have a positive sense of self-value and an appreciation of our own situation and our own qualities, it is very hard to rejoice in another's. If within us is a lack of contentment and well-being then we may easily harbour uncomfortable feelings of envy or resentment towards those we feel are more fortunate. When someone then tells us of something very positive in their life, instead of feeling the warm glow of how wonderful that is, we can easily contract our heart, closing us off from a sense of joy. If we become caught in a negative, depressive attitude towards our life, we may feel things are not fair or that we never have what we want. This unhappy mind can be extremely difficult to remedy without beginning to find a place of acceptance. From acceptance, if we then begin to look at what we do have in our life, we may shift towards a more positive sense of gratitude.

I have always been inspired by those whose lives seem very simple and who are living in relatively humble circumstances with few possessions and yet have a great sense of contentment and joy. This is in contrast to those who are materially incredibly fortunate and yet have an underlying sense of dissatisfaction and unhappiness. I recall Lama Yeshe making the comment many years ago that, for many of us, our difficulty is that we don't know how to enjoy ourselves. This seemed like an extraordinary thing for a Buddhist teacher to say. He was indicating, however, that when we experience things in our life that are potentially pleasurable and satisfying, our tendency is, in his words, to "turn them into *kaka*". (I don't think this word needs translating.) He saw that, because of our dissatisfied and grasping mind, we do not allow things to be as they are with a sense of contentment; we want more and more. This restless, grasping dissatisfaction means we seldom feel a deep sense of satisfaction and enjoyment. He was also implying that inner satisfaction and contentment will give us the capacity to see the world and those around us with a greater feeling of appreciation and joy.

Joy is an energy that comes from deep within, enabling us to maintain a positive, hopeful relationship to life even when things are not easy. Some people have a very natural sense of joy that enables them to remain positive and buoyant even when things are falling apart. For many of us, however, this is not so easy – especially when we are continually bombarded with endless news about the disasters arising in the world around us. Life can then begin to feel very bleak, and our capacity for a more positive outlook can become seriously eroded. But when we have an inner resource of satisfaction, contentment and joy, we can see life in a positive way and we can also share that with others. In troubled times a bodhisattva needs this capacity to be a steady, positive, encouraging presence for others. To rejoice in another's experience, and to appreciate and encourage them fully in who they are, is a wonderful gift to offer. To greet someone with a sense of joy and consideration is a simple gesture of care and kindness that can have a huge effect. To smile at someone can shift their energy. To offer gratitude and appreciation can lift someone's day. Small expressions of a positive heart affect our world in subtle ways.

As we begin to awaken the energy of joy within, it can powerfully affect the world around us even though we do not always recognise it. We are often very aware when someone is grumpy and irritable or negative and complaining. We can feel how their energy emanates and affects our environment. If on the other hand we can begin to emanate the energy of joy and optimism it will have a much more enlivening and enriching effect on our life and the lives of others. Within our subtle-body is a natural potential for the energy of joy and bliss. In the tantric tradition, this energy is at the very core of our being and is a source of health, vitality and inspiration. It is the energy that comes when we feel aligned and engaged with something that deeply connects us to the essence of our true nature. I recall Joseph Campbell once saying that we should "follow our bliss"; we should respond to what brings us joy. Shantideva also spoke of the cultivation of enthusiasm to engage in the things that are meaningful and to have the capacity to rejoice in a task well done.[4] When our creative energies are aligned and able to manifest through how we are in our life, we will increasingly experience satisfaction, joy and, potentially, bliss. In Tarthang Tulku's book *The Joy of Being*,[5] he says that through the practice of the exercises of *Kum Nye* the energy in our body becomes more fluid and free, releasing the natural quality of joy that is in our nature. This feeling can then be expressed in how we respond to others to also bring them joy, enthusiasm, encouragement and appreciation. We will then naturally be able to emanate a sense of joy and gladness when we see others enjoying themselves and living fulfilling lives.

The brahmavihara of limitless joy is a feeling that we can emanate towards all life. As I have said in relation to compassion and love, joy also comes from a mind that is not contracted and tight, but open and spacious. When we are able to free ourselves from this contraction and open to our mind's innate, spacious clarity and awareness, joy will be a natural outflow. This is an attribute of our mind's pristine nature, which is not true of the more negative and dissatisfied feeling often present within our narrow, ordinary dualistic mind. Joy grows as we let go of our narrow attitude to our life and open to a bigger awareness – even when circumstances are challenging.

An area of life that I feel also needs to be part of that bigger awareness is our relationship to the land. We should not underestimate the nourishment and joy we get from an appreciation for the natural environment. To feel elation for the wonder of the natural life on this planet and for its extraordinary beauty is an important way of rejoicing. To feel gratitude for the planet and all that we receive from it is very necessary at a time when we are sorely needing to change our relationship. When I go out into the beautiful land around my home I am often filled with such joy that it can move me to tears. When we become nourished by the joy felt in relationship to the natural world we can then also shift this to an appreciation of others. If we generate a more positive inner feeling that is satisfying, this can give us a sense of richness within that we can share with others. Joy then becomes a much more natural outward expression.

However, joy can also lead to sadness if we are touched by something that moves us deeply. When something or someone becomes deeply meaningful to us, bringing us great joy, we can also have a kind of overinvestment. Such an overinvestment has the potential to lead to a sense of expectation and contraction, and then we want things to remain a certain way. This relates to Lama Yeshe's remark about not knowing how to really enjoy. The joy I experience in relationship to the land I love so much can, if I am not careful, turn to sadness and pain when I see potential damage being done. When we have an expectation, it can lead us away from the joy and move us towards a sense of sadness or disappointment.

Our contraction around what leads to joy can lead us not only to sorrow, but also to excitement. The energy of joy can easily turn to excitement if we begin to be attached to it and ride upon it. I have experienced this in the context of meditation retreats where I felt a growing sense of joy and bliss that I began to contract around and gradually turned the energy into a bubbling sense of excitement. I was once leading a group retreat where, over a period of several weeks, many of those attending were beginning to touch into a quality of energy that was potentially quite joyful, even blissful. For me, the one attempting to hold the boundaries of a silent retreat, what became incredibly problematic was that this joyful energy became very volatile and many in the group could not stop themselves from excitedly chattering together. In my own experience of this in retreat, turning the energy of joy into excitement often led to a sense of depression the following day as my energy crashed. Longchenpa expressed that when we begin to turn joy into a form of either excitement or disappointment, we need to bring in the quality of equanimity to restore a sense of balance (see Figure 3).

Joy is a natural positive outflow of energy that can arise in our nature when we allow ourselves to open rather than contract. The brahmavihara of immeasurable joy arises from an inner spaciousness and emptiness that liberates us from the bondage of suffering. From this the wish arises that all others might also be free of the bondage of suffering in life and experience the joy of complete liberation. This wish leads naturally to the intention of bodhicitta as is reflected in the Tibetan verse of immeasurable joy:

How wonderful it would be if all beings were never separated from the joy of liberation.
May they never be separated from this joy,
May I enable them never to be separated from this joy,
Please bless me all you buddhas to be able to do this.

4

Equanimity

THE FOURTH BRAHMAVIHARA is equanimity, but leaving it till last does not mean it is any less significant than the others. In some respects, one can see equanimity as the ground within which the other three can grow. In fact, within the traditional practices associated with what is called the "six causes and one effect"[6], a meditation process for cultivating bodhicitta, equanimity is at the very beginning. The reason for this is that without the even ground of equanimity, there are not the conditions for the other qualities to grow. If we consider what the opposite of equanimity is, we can see why this might be the case.

From a psychological perspective, when our mind is caught up in all kinds of reactions, judgements and prejudices towards others, then it is very difficult to cultivate compassion and love. For example, when I harbour feelings of resentment or aversion towards someone, it creates a relationship that will not easily turn to one of love and compassion. Negative responses and reactions cloud our capacity to become close and open to another. Certain very positive responses to another may equally distort how we see them. If we have feelings of need or desire towards someone it can also blur our view. Or we may have a feeling of indifference towards others because they are of little significance in our life and do not particularly interest us. So long as we have these kinds of biases towards others, we will find it extremely difficult to have the balance of mind that can begin to open to how someone actually is.

If we look at this more closely, we can observe that the way we see another is very bound up in what we project onto them. When we project negative judgements and prejudices or feelings of fear and repulsion towards someone, then we are not seeing them as they really are. We will not easily see that they also have their qualities and their difficulties and are suffering in different ways just as we are. We are not really aware of this because our mind's primary preoccupation is with what we dislike or find difficult. We will not recognise, for example, that this person probably has friends who really appreciate them and value them in various ways. Our biased view, however, can become very entrenched and hard to overcome. Because it is a projection, this colours our view so strongly that we really believe what we are seeing to be true. From a Jungian perspective this is almost certainly because what is being activated is an aspect of our shadow. According to Jung, what we are unconscious of in ourselves tends to be projected outside. He considered the shadow to hold those aspects of ourselves and those reactions that have been driven into the unconscious because they are unacceptable to us. It may be our fear or insecurity when we are threatened by how or who someone is. It may be that we are irritated or angered because the person touches something in us that is hard to tolerate. We may feel repulsion to the way someone is because of something we are very uncomfortable with in ourselves. We may have been reminded of a situation or experience that was quite traumatic for us and we cannot bear to feel those feelings.

The implication of these experiences is that something is stimulated in our unconscious that we are projecting onto the other person or groups of people. We see this very clearly in our collective experience of those whom we fear as the *other*. This "other" has varied throughout our history and has often been based on race, religion or gender. Today our society often splits into oppositional biases that lead one section of a population to judge, reject and vilify another because they do not hold the same values or views. When we do this we no longer see who they actually are; instead we see them as embodying something we fear or hate. If I feel threatened by someone, it may not be because of the way a person is but rather what they embody for me. Whenever we have these kinds of reactions we need to be careful of our perception because it can be very distorted. When our perception is distorted we lose our objectivity and begin to really believe that what we are seeing is true. Then we are no longer able to make a connection to the other person's actual experience and their reality. From this place there is little capacity for either love or compassion. In the UK we have encountered this in recent years through the process of Brexit, in relation to migrants, with Muslims, and during the pandemic with those who are vaccine hesitant. It is as though our collective need is to have someone to revile and scapegoat.

If I am so bound up in my own reactions, prejudices and projections, I will be unable to see how much the other person is struggling or suffering. Because our negative

biases blind us, I may also be completely unable to
appreciate their qualities and abilities. (It may be helpful
to explore this negative bias in the equanimity meditation
I describe in the Appendix.) We can also see that the same
can and does happen with positive bias. On many
occasions I have seen positive bias lead to problems. An
example of this is when someone has a close friend who is
very loving, caring and considerate, who always seems to
be willing to listen to what they are going through and
responds with care and support. When they begin to see
this person as a very special, precious and loving friend, a
degree of need and expectation grows. This is partly
because the friend satisfies a deep need for love and
attention. The tendency to idealise under these
circumstances also grows, especially when this friend
seems so selfless and caring. If we have such a dear friend,
we may not be aware of how much we begin to project
some inner need, expectation and idealisation onto them.
Positive bias clouds our capacity to see the other as they
really are – with all their needs and struggles.

Such a situation of positive bias may go on for a long
time until something breaks the spell. Perhaps the other
person gets sick or can't be there for us because of their
own needs. Or perhaps they decide that they have had
enough and don't want to always be there as a caring
mother to us. A problem arises because of this change in
habit or attitude: we may find it unbearable. It may bring
feelings of abandonment or rejection that can easily lead
to a sudden switch from closest, dearest friend to hated,
rejected enemy. Unfortunately, in the context of
psychotherapy, I have heard this scenario acted out many
times in relationships where there is an unconscious
projection of needs and expectations upon another. When

this breaks down, the result can be devastating to the relationship and it is extremely hard to repair.

When we have biased views, we will always struggle to allow others to be truly how they are. The cultivation of equanimity begins to bring us back to a place where we have less agendas, less projections and less expectations. We could say that we have less bias or attachment towards people in whom we have no particular interest, people we have a kind of indifference towards. But this misses the way in which our mind can be very tricky in response to those who do not interest us or attract us. We do not notice them or can be indifferent to both their suffering and their happiness.

The three poisons, as they are sometimes called in Buddhism − attachment, aversion and ignorance − all play a part in our lack of equanimity. We can see this psychologically in the examples I have given above. Equanimity enables us to be present with a sense of balance, not becoming drawn into reactive positions and projections. It frees others from having to be a certain way to be acceptable to us. It frees them to be able to be themselves without our judgements or agendas. For me as a therapist this has felt extremely important, especially when people have needed to feel safe to be able to tell a terribly painful story. These may be stories of how shameful they feel about something that happened to them or that they did. It may be people wanting to express their deepest fears or feelings of despair and know that it will be allowed to be as it is without agendas.

Equanimity allows a deep sense of safety because it does not go into dualistic reactions that imply that this is ok but that is not. It enables a relatively neutral ground within which we can begin to make real contact with how someone is and then hold that gently and with openness.

When we are able to sustain this quality of emotional stability and balance, then compassion and love have the space to emerge. As with the other three brahmaviharas, equanimity is a very natural expression of the open, spacious nature of awareness that comes within the practice of mahamudra. When we rest with a spacious and open awareness and do not get caught in subtle reactive tendencies, but rather allow space for whatever appears to be as it is, then equanimity is a natural outcome.

An interesting word of caution from Longchenpa in relation to equanimity concerns when the lack of reaction and bias begins to move towards indifference through ignorance. This can occur when we no longer move into relationship to others because we are not letting ourselves feel real connection. Detachment and an absence of emotional response may then lead to indifference. When this arises, Longchenpa's advice is to restore the sense of connection and relationship that comes from love and the willingness to cherish others.

In a world and at a time when there is so much hostility and division in the form of nationalism, discrimination, prejudice and protectionism, equanimity is a crucial quality. It is, however, one that seems hard for us to cultivate when we are driven by fear and insecurity. We continue to feel the need to protect ourselves and those we feel aligned with and to reject and repel those we fear and hate. So long as we are bound by these biases, we will continue to live in a world of inequality and disharmony where we favour some and reject or scapegoat others. If we could overcome this tendency in our nature, we could live with greater trust in each other – and then with a greater sense of collective safety and security. This is not security that comes from material needs being met, but security that comes from a trust in community and a shared sense of value, equality and respect for all, irrespective of colour, race, gender and religious orientation. If we can begin to have a greater sense of peaceful equanimity in our hearts, then our society can also be more compassionate and loving towards everyone equally. This ground of equanimity is the basis from which bodhicitta will grow and is reflected in the Tibetan verse:

How wonderful it would be if all sentient beings were to abide in peaceful equanimity, free from discriminating attachment and aversion.
May they abide in equanimity,
May I enable them to abide in equanimity,
Please bless me all you buddhas to be able to do this.

*****

At this point we conclude our exploration of the four immeasurables, the four infinite minds. They are an important ground from which the other qualities of bodhicitta arise. Each of us probably has a more natural relationship to one of these four than to the others. We may for example have a relatively easy relationship to compassion but less to love or joy. We may feel a very immediate sense of love and joy but less so with compassion and equanimity. We may feel equanimity very easily but not always the others. This is not a problem; it simply reflects individual differences and shows us the places where it is helpful to go deeper. As we do so, all four can gradually become a natural base for how bodhicitta grows. It is perhaps helpful to see the four as a natural circulation where we move around them and through them dependent upon circumstances. Some circumstances will enhance our compassion, others our joy and still others our sense of love or equanimity. In this way we discover how they feed into each other as a natural expression of our relationships unfolding.

5

Courage

IT IS NO COINCIDENCE that the word "courage" is derived from the old French word *corage*, "heart feeling". Bodhicitta has often been translated as the "awakening heart", "heart mind" or "heart essence" because our relationship to the heart is very central to how we understand its qualities. In English we have a variety of interesting terms associated with the heart. We may use the phrase "to put one's heart into it" or "to be wholehearted" when referring to how we engage with something we are doing. We may similarly express the sense of being "half-hearted" or "losing heart" when we find we are unable to commit to something.

If we are to engage with the bodhisattva's intention of bodhicitta, we must do so wholeheartedly. When we begin to step into the sense of commitment to the path of a bodhisattva we may at first have some understandable hesitation or reservations. This can feel like a significant and profound step to make on our spiritual journey and is one that should not be taken lightly or half-heartedly. As with any task we might embark upon in our life, if we are not fully committed and our sense of motivation is ambivalent, the effect on us can be problematic. As Shantideva emphasises in the chapter on enthusiasm[7] in his *Guide to the Bodhisattva's Way of Life*, when we embark upon a task without a clear intention we may lose heart and never complete what we set out to do. When this happens, he says, other tasks will also be affected because it reinforces the habit of not completing things. He also suggests that we can easily give up when things become difficult or challenging. According to Shantideva, it is considered a major downfall for a bodhisattva to act in this way because, as a result, countless sentient beings will suffer.[8]

We all know how difficult it can be if we are about to embark upon a project when our heart is not really in it. For example, we may be fearful of some aspect of what we are about to do. I recall feeling this when my wife, Anna, and I began to talk about having children. I was very afraid that children would impact my life in a way that could damage my spiritual progress. This was a message I had received some years earlier from teachers who constantly emphasised that the only way to really practice the Dharma was to be a monk and that one would never get enlightened if one had children. This view, conveyed with such authority, had a powerful impact on my decision. I had a huge ambivalence that meant I struggled to engage wholeheartedly with the reality of it. It led to an excruciating inner conflict that only began to change after some years of being a father. I then began to discover that, actually, being a parent was probably teaching me more about compassion, love and letting go of self than being a monk ever would.

Another reason we may have resistance to engage in and enter into a process wholeheartedly may be because we do not believe we can really do what is asked of us. This can be especially true when we consider the path of the bodhisattva. In my early years as a Tibetan Buddhist I recall a teacher emphasising that a bodhisattva is willing to go into the hell realms in order to liberate beings from suffering. At the time I remember thinking, "I would never have the courage to do that". It led me to feel that bodhicitta and the life of the bodhisattva were way beyond my capacity. Fortunately, Lama Yeshe was very reassuring when he would describe us as "baby bodhisattvas" who of course couldn't do that. The point is to grow in capacity.

Bodhicitta brings us to gradually develop our capacity to bear the challenges and hardships of an extraordinary path. The bodhisattva vow includes the line "to practice the stages of graded development exactly as all bodhisattvas have done"[9]. This does not imply that we are all perfect and fully accomplished right from the start. It means that our capacity to engage with the life that seeks to serve the welfare of others grows gradually. One of the principle things that helps in this process is to step into it with a sense of wholeheartedness, to be willing to take up the challenge. This requires a level of courage. This courage recognises that a choice we make in this journey is to *engage with life* and its struggles as well as its joys – not run away from it. A bodhisattva goes beyond the attitude that wants to avoid or "abandon the happiness of this life", as some Tibetans call it, and instead remains in this world for the welfare of others. But this life is far from easy and rather than being full of pleasurable experiences that we should renounce, for many there can be a sense of drowning in the struggle. We live in a world and at a time where there is a great deal of fear, insecurity and stress. It may be tempting to think we can follow a path that leads to liberation and peace, and such a path is certainly present within the Buddhist tradition. A bodhisattva, however, makes a choice to remain within an embodied life in order to serve the greater good. This requires a level of courage and commitment that must be wholehearted.

It is often said in the teachings that a bodhisattva transforms adverse circumstances into the path of awakening. To do this we must grow the capacity and have the willingness and courage to take up the challenge. There is a strength that grows from this process as though we gradually develop the emotional muscle to deal with and tolerate what we meet on the journey. As I said in the introduction, the term bodhisattva can be translated as the "awakening warrior". It is this warrior-like attitude that does not recoil from the challenges of the path which enables a bodhisattva's capacity to grow. When I first began to practice as a psychotherapist, I was not sure that I would be able to cope with certain things that clients might bring into the therapeutic space. Over the years, however, I grew to be able to cope with more of the pain and suffering some of my clients expressed. As my capacity grew, I could hold their suffering with much greater confidence and trust in the process that was unfolding. I learned that I was not going to be able to solve their problems or take their pain away but I could bear being with them as they went through awful experiences.

I recall H.H. Dalai Lama saying some years ago that a bodhisattva needs a strong ego to be able to liberate others from suffering. Many of us were a bit shocked that he should say this in view of the apparent emphasis in Buddhism on getting rid of the ego. What he was saying, however, is that we do need a relative self and that sense of self needs to be stable, steady and robust enough to cope with the challenges the path brings. It is not easy to live in the world and serve others. When we are psychologically unstable or our sense of self is emotionally wounded and therefore fragile and vulnerable, it is very hard to expect ourselves to take on the challenge of a bodhisattva's way of life. We need to first heal some of our own inner wounding to prepare the ground. Once some of this wounding is healed and we have a relatively healthy and stable sense of self, we can begin to take on the challenge. As we then consider stepping across the threshold into the life of a bodhisattva, we need to do so with a steadiness and self-confidence that is grounded and balanced.

At some point in this journey we may choose to take the bodhisattva vow or vows. This process is a step towards a new way of seeing our life. It consolidates a sense of meaning to our life that may have already been there, and through taking a vow we are making our intention clear. We make an inner decision to maintain a life dedicated to the welfare of others. This step may feel somewhat daunting at first if we understand its implications. As we make this inner commitment, however, it means that we begin a journey of discovery and learning during which we gradually come to embody a bodhisattva's qualities. When we take the bodhisattva vow, it is witnessed by all the buddhas and bodhisattvas and we have their support and encouragement. This is something we do with great sincerity and with the knowledge that our journey is just beginning.

We could say that a bodhisattva lives between worlds, remaining in the world of form and embodiment while opening to the clarity and luminosity of our innate buddha potential. This means living with a growing awareness of our pristine nature that is free of the struggles of being entangled in the world while choosing to remain within it.

This is not a path of disembodied spiritual transcendence. The choice to live between realities requires a commitment, dedication and the courage to remain embodied while being a vehicle for our buddha-nature to manifest in the world for the welfare of others.

6
Big Mind

LAMA YESHE used the phrase *big mind* to refer to a certain attitude he felt we need to have when we cultivate bodhicitta. He used the term in relation to a tendency that many of us students had to be small-minded. I think we all can recognise our small-mindedness and how uncomfortable it can be. This small mind grows out of our disposition to contract around our sense of self. It is a disposition to be narrow, constricted and uptight in our attitude towards things that seem important to us in our life. Narrow-mindedness can take on so many forms in limiting our views, whether within our relationships, our work, our beliefs, or our prejudices and judgements towards others in our society. Possibly the most destructive narrowing of our mind is when we have fixed judgements about others in a way that breeds hostility and prejudice. We see the consequences of this in many ways in our contemporary world. We may find ourselves holding disparaging views about Black people, Muslims, gays, immigrants or other communities. Such prejudice can and does lead to scapegoating, abuse and violence.

The small mind gets fixed on small things and makes them seem very important. In our relationships this can become a source of so much argument and bickering. Little things become irritating and annoying; we can end up fighting over things that are not significant and yet seem so at the time. Our small-mindedness can mean that we fail to recognise a bigger picture that is around us. I recall a very striking experience of this in March 2011 following the tsunami that destroyed the lives of hundreds of people in Japan. Soon after this shocking event, on the television there were frequent films of the damage and destruction the tsunami had caused. During this period several of my psychotherapy clients came to talk about problems in their life that were creating friction with their partners. As they were speaking, it became clear to them how insignificant their difficulties were when they placed their problems alongside the lives of those in Japan. They suddenly opened their minds to a much bigger picture which enabled them to let go of what had been preoccupying them. At the very least it put their problems into perspective.

Central to many of the teachings given by Tibetans on the cultivation of bodhicitta is the need to let go of the preoccupation caught up just in our own suffering and begin to open to the suffering of others. As I wrote in the chapter on love, Tibetans often say that we are caught in "self-cherishing" and that this is the root of all of our suffering. I don't find this expression particularly helpful because it can imply that taking care of ourselves or looking after ourselves is bad. As Westerners, many of us need to begin to take care of ourselves in a positive and kind way, especially when our sense of self-value or self-regard can be so damaged. A more helpful term than "self-cherishing" is "self-preoccupation" – and indeed many of us are very self-preoccupied because we are psychologically wounded in some way. If I feel bad about myself and have low self-esteem, one of the consequences can be a kind of self-preoccupation.

If we are to cultivate bodhicitta, it is very necessary to gradually release this self-preoccupation. We can then begin to open our awareness to be more sensitive, considerate and empathic towards the suffering of others. We can only do this if we begin to heal the wounded sense of self that causes the self-preoccupation. Essential in this process is the cultivation of greater self-compassion and self-acceptance so that we can naturally let go of the contracted preoccupation and open to others.

Our small-mindedness arises for a reason and doesn't immediately and automatically disappear when we are given the message that we have to consider others more than self. Healing our sense of self can enable the process of change. Then we need to notice all the habits in our life that lead us to contract into such a narrow, limiting attitude. We change these habits, in part, by becoming much more conscious of their presence. We can also change by cultivating a capacity within meditation to relax the contraction in our body, our emotional life and our mind. This contraction is a strong tendency that reacts instinctually when something pushes our buttons. If we pay attention, we will be able to feel contraction in the body. Although we may be most familiar with the idea of attachment or grasping, in terms of our embodied and felt sense there is a definite contraction that tightens and freezes our experience. From one perspective we could say that this habitual tendency to contract is the root of suffering. When we contract, we lose the capacity to respond to life situations with openness and fluidity.

For our quality of bodhicitta to grow, we need to gradually shift from our narrow, limited mind tendency, caught up in a small perspective, to a much broader, more expansive view. This view opens us to an awareness of the presence of countless others who live with us upon this planet and whose lives are often full of suffering. Bodhicitta is sometimes described as the desire to liberate *all* beings from suffering. This perspective leads us to recognise the vastness of life in all its forms and to take on a sense of what H.H. Dalai Lama has called "universal responsibility and big heart". Universal responsibility is not something we can suddenly take on from an ordinary sense of self. To do so would almost certainly lead to a kind of messianic inflation. Ultimately it will require that we shift from our narrow ego-centred reality to a recognition of our spacious, empty nature. Then we let go of the identification with a solid sense of self and open to the quality of a bigger awareness that is beyond self, beyond identity. This is the nature of what is sometimes called "ultimate bodhicitta", the spacious awareness of clarity and emptiness.

Cultivating spacious awareness within the practice of meditation is central to the practice of *mahamudra*. In this practice, with time, a natural capacity grows to rest with a deep sense of spaciousness and clarity. This allows whatever is arising, in both the body and mind, the space to be as it is and to move through. Emotions and feelings arise within the space of awareness and, rather than contracting into them, we allow them to pass through without reaction. As we cultivate this natural, spacious clarity and empty awareness we are truly beginning to experience big mind. This is the innate nature of the mind that is always there but often obscured or obstructed by the habitual tendency of our narrow, small, dualistic mind.

We should not underestimate the significance of this shift from our small ego-identity mind to the vast openness of awareness that needs to be present in the emergence of bodhicitta. This openness of mind enables us to sustain a ground of balance and steadiness in the face of the challenges of a bodhisattva's life. When something impacts us in our relationship to life and how we hold the welfare of others, this steady ground of open awareness gives us the freedom to let go and maintain a sense of balance and spaciousness. I recall once reading something the Indian scholar Nagarjuna[10] wrote, that a bodhisattva does not get into conflict because they are able to refrain from holding onto any position as an ultimate truth. I feel that this is of great importance in a world where people feel the need to hold onto positions, beliefs, attitudes and opinions that inevitably come into conflict and opposition.

When we cultivate a big mind, we can more readily let go of dualistic positions held as if they were truths and instead maintain greater balance and freedom. Recently in the UK there have been some extremely contentious political issues that many people have very rigid views about. I have found it very liberating to let go of this tendency and not become caught up in the belief that my position is right. In relationship to the Dharma, I have also needed to let go of narrow or fixed ideas of what Buddhist life may be like in the West and instead allow something much more organic to grow. This has felt important in terms of integrating what has been my relationship to a Tibetan tradition in Western life. It has also felt crucial in supporting others in this process.

A big mind allows whatever needs to unfold to unfold and transform, whereas a small, tight mind becomes stuck in prescriptions, positions and beliefs that require things to be a certain way. A narrow mind is often uncomfortable with change and holds on for security and safety. It wants to have control. Having a spacious, open mind means not having agendas and not always needing to know how things will unfold. There is something very creative about this willingness to then live with uncertainty and mystery. The spacious and open nature of awareness that is big mind enables a bodhisattva to live in times when there is greater uncertainty – without becoming caught up in an environment of stress, insecurity and fear. At the current time in history, political and economic uncertainty as well as the presence of a pandemic fill people's lives with stress and fear. Perhaps at times like this a bodhisattva's capacity to rest with a more spacious and balanced awareness can also be a resource for others. We can be a better resource than when we become caught up in reactive fears and anxieties that come from the narrow and contracted sense of self.

The gradual awakening of spacious awareness, implicit in the idea of big mind, leads us towards an appreciation of the quality of mind that is present in our buddha potential. Our buddha-nature has always had the innate quality of primordially pure clarity of empty awareness, but this quality is veiled from us. This is the ultimate nature of our mind that will awaken as we clear the veil. Once we begin to recognise this clarity and awareness within ourselves, we gain a deeper and deeper capacity to let go and open. Throughout our day we gradually become more able to rest in this quality of spacious awareness and not be so entangled in the potential emotional reactivity of our relationships. This in turn makes us more able to respond to another with clarity, presence and openness and allow them to be as they are. Our quality of compassion and love will have a natural spaciousness that is free of personal agendas and projections. We will be able to respond to the suffering of others in a more open and spacious way. Working as a psychotherapist, I have found this clarity and spaciousness to be a profound way of being with clients to hold them and be present with whatever they bring into the therapeutic space. The combination of spacious clarity and compassion gives us the potential to be with another's suffering in a way that deeply supports their healing and transformation. When someone is in distress, perhaps the greatest gift we can give is this spacious, compassionate presence.

7

Surrender

FOR MUCH OF OUR EARLY ADULT LIFE, our ego is an important central focus of how we engage with the world. As we grow up, our "identity project", as Michael Washburn[11] calls it, is a necessary aspect of our journey. In the West, particularly, we live in a world that requires that we become self-reliant, self-sustaining individuals in a society that is competitive, insecure and often relatively hazardous. We must develop the capacity to survive in this world and also, if possible, to actually flourish within it. In view of this it is not surprising that we all are impacted, in varying degrees, by the pressure and stress that this places upon our ordinary sense of self. As a psychotherapist I have worked for years with those who have struggled within this life process and who have sought help to find a more healthy way to be with it. What becomes clear in the therapeutic context is that we are seldom to blame for the suffering we experience; we are all on one level the victims of a relentless and, sadly, dysfunctional human world. We may have made choices along the way that were not helpful. We may also have got into ways of being that have protected us but which are often found to be destructive in the long run. A phrase that recurs in Buddhism is that we are all seeking happiness and to be free of suffering, but the problem is that we do not truly understand what does lead to happiness and instead continually create the causes for suffering.

Having said this, the extraordinary thing is that most of us do actually survive and to some degree create something of our lives that can be fulfilling. Our ego-identity project is a necessary process in much of our life as we find the capacity to live in our world.

During this process many of us find ourselves "called" to look more deeply into ourselves and start to touch into another level of being. We may see this as a spiritual calling if we wish to use that language. Many of us start to question the meaningfulness of the materialistic way we live our lives and begin to look for something deeper. Those of us who respond to this calling and begin to explore the path of Buddhism may then discover something extraordinary. The message that had huge impact for me personally, as I began to study the Tibetan tradition, was that my innate nature was essentially pure and clear but was obscured and therefore not easy to touch. Rather than thinking that my true nature was sinful and bad, I learned that actually my true nature was "clean clear", to use Lama Yeshe's words. It was this growing awareness that subsequently led me on a journey of study and meditation to hopefully come closer to experiencing that buddha-nature.

During my studies, bodhicitta was always emphasised as the intention to become a buddha for the welfare of sentient beings. In response to that message, my natural tendency was to apply myself to the path in the same way

I had approached my life. I felt that if I was diligent and sincere I could cultivate the qualities spoken of along the path. I was very motivated and encouraged by teachers that emphasised that if we do apply ourselves then the realisations of the path are all possible. There was constant emphasis that we should work hard to accumulate merit in order to get enlightened. This was often underscored by the converse, that to not practice would lead to ever more suffering and potential rebirth in lower states of being. This made me very motivated, and as a consequence I eventually went into long retreat with the understanding that meditation was vital in this process of awakening.

Bodhicitta was always a very important part of this motivation, albeit in a somewhat intellectual way. I was, I believed, dedicated to a path of awakening for the welfare of others. I tried very hard in my retreats to practice as skilfully as possible, but at some point I began to question the entire basis upon which I was practicing. I began to feel that the constant attempt to gather merit was just another form of self-interest. I was sincere and dedicated, but still felt I was motivated very much from a place of my ego. I began to see that my Buddhist practice had become yet another "identity project". I may have shifted from a "worldly" project to a "spiritual" one, but it was still an identity project. I began to feel disappointed and frustrated as though I was getting something wrong, especially with my ideas of what I believed bodhicitta, as a quality of intention, should be.

At one point in my retreat I was translating a text on the practice I was doing and a particular line stood out to me. When I stopped and really connected to what it was saying, something in me was suddenly woken up. The line was, "in order to liberate sentient beings from suffering, I offer myself immediately to all the buddhas."[12]

Suddenly I could see that I was approaching this entire path from the wrong perspective. I had been trying so hard to achieve something that was alluding me and then finally now I could see that from my ego's place I could not go on. I suddenly saw that bodhicitta was not about "I must get enlightened for the sake of sentient beings" because there was an inherent contradiction in that very thought. I saw that I needed to make a very subtle yet profound shift from "I will" to "Thy will be done". I was aware that, technically speaking, there is no *Thy* in Buddhism as an ultimate godhead. But I saw that if I was to truly understand and trust in the presence of the buddhas, then they would be there - and are there - to enable me to unfold.

This brings me to the meaning of surrender within the context of Buddhism, and of bodhicitta in particular. As an aspect of bodhicitta we need to begin to let go of the striving ego that seeks to attain something and instead give ourselves up. We could say we give up, but not in the sense of being defeated. It is rather that we give up the striving and trying that does not accomplish what we seek. Rather than being oriented towards a goal, we come back to the present and open to let go and be guided. In this sense it is a realignment of our intention, recognising that to awaken we have to give up what obstructs our awakening, namely our ego-identity project. As we surrender we may not know exactly how things are going to unfold but we remain open and responsive to what evolves. Often I simply have the inner feeling that, in the things I do, I do not need to have some goal in mind but simply the willingness to let it unfold and trust in the process.

Central to this sense of surrender is what Jung would have called the Self, or what in Buddhism we could call our buddha-nature. Jung recognised that an aspect of the process of individuation is that at some point the ego begins to give way to the Self as the central agent of transformation. As the ego begins to let go and open to the natural way in which the Self "guides" us and unfolds us, we gain a deeper level of understanding and wisdom. It is as though the Self embodies what might be seen as the inner guru when we can listen to its insights and surrender to its guidance.

Translated into Buddhist language, if I begin to align myself with my innate buddha-nature then this will be the inner guide that awakens me on the path. The hazard within the Buddhist tradition is that we often project this inner potential onto an outer person and turn them into the "guru". This may prove satisfactory for a while if the outer person is trustworthy and carries our projection skilfully. But this projection has many risks and can often lead to disappointment, when the guru fails to live up to our ideals, or to a kind of devotional bind that blinds us to our innate potential. Many people have suffered the former of these outcomes and then have had to rebuild their spiritual life in a less naive way. Others, who become caught in devotional idealism, can easily find themselves in a cult-like situation surrounded by an entire culture that seeks to perpetuate the illusion of the guru's ultimate unquestionable authority.

Surrender in this form is not the surrender I am referring to here. The surrender that is needed in the emergence of bodhicitta, within the process of individuation, is the surrender to something deeper that is also in our nature. We surrender to the unfolding of our buddha-nature and how that is inseparable from the true nature of all the buddhas. With this attitude we allow ourselves to be transformed and trust in that process. Surrender is also where we recognise that once bodhicitta is there in the very ground of our lives, it becomes like a river that is flowing through our life. We step into that river and allow it to take us where it needs to go. Ultimately the river leads to the ocean of full awakening, but we do not have to try and make that happen.

As we do this, we also need to recognise our responsibility in the process. A phrase from the Middle East comes to mind: "Put your trust in God but don't forget to tether your camel." Although we make the shift from I will to Thy will be done, we still have a responsibility to engage with the process. Our ordinary ego and its quality of will is still responsible for engaging in life and the tasks we take on, but that will is aligned with a greater will. It is interesting that in the teachings on bodhicitta a quality is described which is sometimes called the "Great Will". It is a quality of will that moves us and is no longer personal, but arises as a powerful force that comes through us because we are aligned with the "Source", with buddha-nature. We surrender to this Great Will and, in doing so, align our own personal sense of intention to engage in our life for the welfare of others. What then emerges as we respond in this way may totally surprise us when life circumstances enable things to unfold with less struggle and greater ease. When we feel aligned in this way, we can begin to let go and allow what emerges to emerge. Bodhicitta becomes a natural expression of that process unfolding.

Ways to Surrender

There are certain practices that can help us in the process of surrender. Perhaps the most obvious of these is the prostration. While traditionally this is seen as a practice used for purification within what is called the *ngöngdro* or preliminary practice, the prostration can also be a profound process of surrender if we know how to approach it. What enables this to be effective is how we cultivate an inner attitude as we prostrate.

It may be helpful to briefly describe the process of prostration in relation to the experience of surrender. There are several variations on the theme of prostration, ranging from simply holding palms together at the heart to the long prostration where one stretches out on the floor. What I will describe here could be consistent with any prostration style.

To begin we need to invite into the space the presence of the buddhas in some form. This may be a chosen deity with whom we have a particular heart connection, or it could be the presence of the buddhas more generally. Note that I am not suggesting the presence of a physical guru or lama because, as I have said, this is not the orientation of surrender I wish to endorse. With the presence of the buddhas we stand and spend some time tuning into the awareness that we are wishing to aid sentient beings in the most beneficial way we can. To do so we need the support and guidance of the buddhas because we are limited from the perspective of our ordinary self. With a heartfelt openness to receive the blessings of the buddhas, we feel the sense of surrender. I find the phrase I have mentioned before helps in this: "In order to benefit sentient beings, I offer myself immediately to all the buddhas." We need to also recall that, as we consider the buddhas, we are also making a connection between their external presence and the relationship to our own innate buddha-nature. We need to deeply understand that these two are inseparable.

The physical action is to place the palms together and bring them to the crown, to the forehead, down to the throat, and to the heart. As we do this it can also be helpful to have the sense that we are receiving blessings that flow down from the crown. We then either kneel down to touch our forehead onto the floor, in what is called the seven-point prostration, or we do the long prostration. With the latter we stretch out onto the floor and then finally place the palms together in front of the head. As we lie on the floor we have in our awareness a deep sense of letting ourselves surrender and open. We offer ourselves to the buddhas to receive their holding guidance and blessing, which can be imagined in the form of light descending into the body.

A second practice that can also be very helpful in the cultivation of our capacity to surrender is known as the mandala offering. Here we create an offering that includes all that we are in our life and then present it to the buddhas. This will mean gradually building a visualisation of the aspects of our life that make up our reality in relation to both inner and outer processes. Traditionally one would actually create a physical offering and then present it to the buddhas. In *Preparing for Tantra*[13] and *The Mandala and Visions of Wholeness*[14] I have described this in more detail and also provided a Western form of the offering that can be more personal than the traditional verses that are recited.

When this ritual is performed with the physical offering, a specific construction of a mandala requires a traditionally crafted offering set. It is however easy to make an offering without this traditional kit. We need to find a bowl that we hold as valuable or beautiful. We then gather together rice and some precious or semi-precious stones or jewellery as the substance of the offering. We then sit and invite the presence of the buddhas into the space in a similar way to the prostration. We gradually cultivate a sense that we are preparing to offer all that we are in our life, including our positive aspects as well as those things we may struggle with. We then gradually fill the bowl with the rice and precious objects as we reflect upon those things we are offering. When complete, we hold the offering and present it to the buddhas with the thought as before: "In order to benefit sentient beings I offer myself immediately to all the buddhas." Having made this offering, we receive the blessings of the buddhas in the form of light.

As we perform these rituals, it is important to be receptive to the idea that we are letting go of the centrality of the ego in our life and are opening to be supported to awaken. This aspect of bodhicitta diminishes the ego's ambition in the process of our spiritual journey, recognising that shift from I will to Thy will be done. There is a question within this of trust, and in what do we trust? A Christian would immediately respond with a sense of trust in the higher power of God. As a Buddhist we do not think in this way. However, if we understand more deeply the nature of the buddhas' awakening then there is also a place of trust. A buddha is not just a physical historical form. Buddha quality is present for us all the time because of the three bodies, or *kayas*, of a buddha. A buddha's mind has awoken to the omniscient wisdom that recognises the empty nature of reality. This quality of mind or quality of awareness is called *dharmakaya*, or wisdom truth body, and is seen as the underlying ground of our reality, beyond form and pervaded by bliss, love and compassion. This aspect of the buddhas is present for us all the time even though we do not easily recognise it. Like the sun behind the clouds, it is there when we open to its presence.

A buddha's energetic nature has also awoken to its full potential when it becomes the pure body of bliss of a buddha known as the *sambhogakaya*. This is sometimes called the indestructible body because it will remain as an energetic presence that, under the right conditions, we can also tune into. Sambhogakaya becomes a source of blessing and inspiration, awakening inner vision that brings an awareness of the ever-presence of the buddhas, especially through the emanation of deities.

These two attributes of buddha activity are always present for us if and when we open to them. It is on this level that we enter into relationship with surrender to the presence, support and guidance of the buddhas. In this we can have a level of trust because we are attuning to or aligning with the innate purity, wisdom and love of buddha-nature. Bringing this relationship into our lives can profoundly affect how we travel the path. The striving and ambition of our ordinary ego-identity project becomes an unnecessary encumbrance once we are ready to let go and surrender.

8

Vision of Wholeness

WHEN I FIRST BEGAN to learn about bodhicitta in my early years as a Tibetan Buddhist, it was always strongly emphasised that the goal of the path was to become a buddha for the sake of others. I began to see this goal as something that I aspired to achieve even though the state of buddhahood seemed like an extraordinarily distant possibility. Though I had learned in theory the nature of a buddha's qualities, they were very much an intellectual, rather abstract notion I could barely comprehend. The intellectual idea of buddhahood, combined with the strong imperative to attain this goal, felt disappointingly unreal and unreachable when I began to practice. I was given the understanding that to achieve this I had to accumulate vast amounts of "merit", or positive karma, cultivated with the right intention, as well as continually purify myself of negative karma. I lived in a community that seemed obsessed with merit in a way that felt far from selfless and hardly dedicated to others. It was a kind of acquisitive attitude that seemed a contradiction to the very essence of what I felt bodhicitta was really about. I was told there were certain days when our merit would multiply millions of times and so they were important days to do good things. Increasingly I began to feel I could not relate to this world that was so determined to strive to become a buddha by accumulating lots of merit. It also made me feel as though my practice was totally bound up in achieving a distant goal rather than genuinely being present and responsive to the moment and to others. I felt that something needed to be very different.

In my time studying to become a Jungian psychotherapist, I saw that Jung's view of the process of individuation had an extraordinary recognition at its heart. When I consider what it was that drew me onto the journey I began to follow, I see that it was not a goal of some sort of perfected state of being. It came from another place in myself. Jung wrote of something that he saw as significant in what calls us to the journey of individuation: a "vision of wholeness". In *Man and His Symbols*[15] Jung brings together two important archetypal principles, the journey and the vision of wholeness. He saw in his own life and his work with others that a vision of wholeness holds a huge importance in our movement towards awakening. He understood that this vision may come in different forms and at different times in our life. He also acknowledged that individuation does not require an intellectual understanding of the meaning of the vision; rather, we are touched by its presence. It speaks to us in a language that our deeper psyche recognises because it connects us to the "Source".

In *The Mandala and Visions of Wholeness* I describe an experience from when I was around eleven that touched me deeply even though I had no idea at the time of its true significance. I had been on a long hike with a friend and ventured onto a forest pathway that eventually led to the side of a lake. To my amazement, in the centre of the lake was a small island upon which stood a Japanese pagoda. At that age I had never seen anything like it before. But it profoundly affected me, and I knew there was something very magical about it even though I had no capacity to put it into words. Even to this day the memory is extremely vivid. From a Jungian perspective, what I saw was a vision of wholeness in the form of an Eastern pagoda.

While Jung acknowledged the effect of such a vision on individuation, from a Buddhist perspective such a depth of experience has a significant effect on our awakening bodhicitta. While bodhicitta is often spoken of in terms of attaining enlightenment or buddhahood, I feel that a deeper resonance comes when I consider awakening to an innate potential – one that is already present within my being. I find that this inner alignment with my own buddha-nature touches me more deeply. I can also instinctively feel that the visions of wholeness that are present within the Buddhist world resonate in a way that does not require intellectual knowledge. I feel I know intuitively.

In my late teens and early twenties, before I knew much about Buddhism, I found that images of the Buddha gave me a deep feeling of comfort. I was fascinated by and drawn towards a quality of stillness and rest that they communicated. Within the tantric tradition in particular we encounter many elaborate images of deities, all of which could be seen as expressions of a vision of wholeness. It is within tantra that we begin to recognise that these visions of wholeness are an emanation of our innate buddha-nature. They are there to bring us into relationship with our potential enlightenment as something we can meet in the present, not as some distant state that we may at some point be able to achieve. It is said that the tantric path of practice "brings the result into the present". This is facilitated by meditating upon deities that embody that resultant quality. While our innate buddha potential may be temporarily veiled from us, it is nevertheless there and has always been so. What we need to do is to begin to clear the veil and awaken to its nature. Developing an awareness of the presence of a deity helps that veil to clear and brings us more closely into alignment with our buddha quality.

If we become more acquainted with the vision of wholeness embodied in a deity, perhaps together with its mandala [16], it changes the nature of our growing experience of bodhicitta. Rather than being an intention to attain some distant goal, bodhicitta is more the recognition that we can awaken to our innate buddha-nature right now for the welfare of others. The vision enables us to open to our true nature, recognising that we can attune to its presence *right now*. This can give us a confidence and sense of empowerment; we recognise that our potential buddhahood is within us now even though it may be veiled. Many years ago, Lama Yeshe would repeatedly remind us of the reality of our "clean, clear totality nature" because many of us had a deeply rooted low sense of self-value which he would call our "low quality nature". He could also see that we would sometimes fall into despondency feeling that buddhahood was impossible to achieve because we were so deluded. His repeated affirmation of our innate nature brought a real sense of joy and encouragement that this was something we could genuinely awaken.

Bodhicitta, when grounded in our buddha-nature, brings us back to the present as an expression of our readiness to awaken to our innate potential and begin to manifest or embody this in the world. We could say that we become a vehicle or vessel for our buddha-nature to come through us in all that we do. As we align ourselves in this way, our experience of bodhicitta energises what we do, enabling us to gradually go beyond our limitations and fully embody our natural human potential.

Within the tantric tradition, this expression of bodhicitta is enhanced by the way we meditate upon a deity. When a particular deity is our primary vision of wholeness, often called our *yidam* or heart deity, we repeatedly attune to this quality in meditation. With time we begin to experience the deity's presence coming through us, bringing a sense of our resultant awakened nature into the present. Our bodhicitta intention is then to increasingly embody this awakened potential in the present moment to serve the welfare of others. This feels very different to the idea of a goal to become a buddha in some uncertain distant time. Understanding this immediacy can empower us to feel more optimistic and more confident in our life. As a bodhisattva engaging in the world we may have a long journey ahead, but we are able to connect to and align with our innate potential in the present.

9

Meaning

I CANNOT BEGIN TO RECALL how many times I have heard some of my Tibetan teachers repeat the phrase "making our life meaningful." Meaning, however, for many of us in the West is a somewhat ambiguous idea. It is not a simple thing to bring meaning into our life, and what may bring meaning for one person may not for another. We may equally say that what may bring meaning at one time in our life may not at another time. As a psychotherapist I often found myself sitting with clients who had descended into a painfully disheartened or even depressed place where they felt their life was meaningless. Sitting with them in this space, I became acutely aware that it didn't help to try and conjure up some fabricated sense of meaning that would alleviate the distress. Meaning does not necessarily come from finding a new job, or starting a training, moving to another country or finding a girlfriend. To be in a place of no meaning may lead to desperate feelings of pointlessness or failure or that life is not worth living. If we learn to open to these feelings without judgement and fear, we can align

ourselves with what can be a natural inner process of
change.

What brings meaning into our life, and how that sense
of meaning actually arises, is perhaps something of a
mystery. It seems that people are often very naturally
drawn to certain experiences that satisfy a need for
meaning. For some, having children brings an
extraordinary sense of meaning. For others it can often be
a project or task that stimulates interest or creative
inspiration. For yet others it can be genuinely caring for
those who are in need of help. What may bring meaning
can even be relatively superficial. Within Buddhist
teachings and scriptures there is often a rather scornful
view of meaning that comes from "worldly life", yet for
many of us, what may bring meaning into aspects of our
life might be considered "worldly." Is this necessarily bad
or wrong? I could not judge. But it is clear that while we
are young it is completely natural to gain meaning through
things related to what I have called our identity project.
This is how our ego identity grows and how we discover
who we are and what our qualities and capacities are as
we enter into the world. Learning a skill or profession may
be profoundly meaningful through certain phases of life;
these should not be judged as worldly just because they are
not obviously "spiritual".

As our life unfolds, the nature of what brings meaning
also evolves. Often this evolution can involve some sense
of disillusionment when what was once meaningful begins
to lose its value. It is this process that I have often seen in
the therapy space when, for example, a person has
dedicated a huge amount of time and energy developing a
business or career and has then become disillusioned. The
classic midlife crisis can be of this nature. Someone may
follow a particular path that has required great

commitment and focus and then at some point the question arises, "What am I doing?" or, "What is the point?" When the bottom drops out of our world in this way, it can be devastating and very frightening. The sense of being adrift, lost, without direction in a wasteland of doubt, fear and uncertainty may be very painful.

At these times, often my role as a therapist is to simply be a witness to the process. I cannot change it or rescue someone in that place. I cannot wave a magic wand and all will be well. It is often a time of waiting and digesting what has happened, grieving the past and what is lost. It is also a time when the solution, if that is what we seek, has to come from within.

Jung spoke of the Self as the centre of our totality but also as the archetype of meaning. Jung saw that the Self expresses its presence within our psyche through visions of wholeness. He also saw that the Self enables us to have an awareness of what can give meaning when we connect to something that becomes "numinous". What he meant is that there are certain things, events or activities in our life that come alive when they touch something deeply within us. When a task or idea suddenly becomes charged with meaning, it does so because it is "touched" by the Self. That is to say there is a kind of connection, like suddenly being plugged in to the mains. We feel energy return. We feel a sense of movement and intention that begins to call us. The something we have connected to becomes numinous, alive, charged.

Meaning cannot be fabricated; it arises in that connection to a sense of interest and inspiration that comes from the Self. What brings this inspiration will change through our life. This is partly a reflection of the Self gradually awakening us to a deeper or higher purpose connected to individuation. From Jung's point of view, individuation is the gradual actualisation of our unique capacity to awaken and respond to a greater imperative for the welfare of all. This is not the same as individualism, which is simply concerned with developing the "small self". In individuation we gradually awaken to our potential wholeness to serve the greater good.

In this respect we could say that individuation is at the heart of the path of the bodhisattva. We could also say that the Buddha's path was an example of individuation: he was able to Self-actualise and awaken his innate potential. Bodhicitta in this respect could be seen as the quality of intention and inspiration that can bring the greatest meaning into our lives. In the *lam rim*, or graduated path, often held to be the clarification of the path to awakening, the path begins with the recognition of what is called our "precious human rebirth". This is the rebirth within the human condition which, because of our buddha-nature, is endowed with the potential to awaken. This human condition has such extraordinary potential and yet is fleeting and transitory. Our death is definite and the actual length of our lifespan most uncertain. It is because of this that we must bring the greatest of meaning into our lives and not waste it on unnecessary "worldly concerns".

This is a powerful argument; I recall in my early days as a Tibetan Buddhist finding this perspective very activating. This activation was enhanced by a second message, that what brings greater meaning to this life is if we can use it to awaken for the welfare of others. Bodhicitta was always placed as the most meaningful way to engage with our life. It felt challenging. This may have been the greatest meaning, but I had to evolve towards that in my own way and my own time. It was as though at first I tried hard to live this view, or intention, but I was not quite ready for it. I still had many of my own issues to resolve before I could truly inhabit this sense of meaning.

While this became a significant aspiration, I needed to do some work upon myself psychologically before I could completely settle into this bodhicitta reality. That did not invalidate its presence in my life; it meant it would gradually become more central. As a source of meaning, bodhicitta is like the river that runs beneath our life. It is as though we align ourselves with its flow and allow it to inform our life, sometimes in an obvious and explicit way. At other times it may recede to be the undercurrent that moves us but not so explicitly. If we trust in this undercurrent and let its meaning inform us on a deep level, then it will shape what we do and where we go. It will increasingly inform how we live our life and the kinds of decisions we make. We may come to times when we see that what we have been engaged in ceases to feel aligned with this undercurrent, and we may choose to change. We may decide to change our job or relationship. We may bring new directions into our life that feel aligned with this root of meaning and that bring us into new alignment.

If we bring together some of the other qualities I have described in earlier chapters with this sense of meaning, we can see for example that surrender is a significant way of engaging with what unfolds. We can see that bringing our vision of wholeness to our sense of meaning will enhance what we do. We need the courage and quality of heart to engage with what is meaningful. We also need to ground this in a heartfelt sense of love and compassion for those we come into relationship with.

Love and compassion are at the root of what is meaningful when we begin to devote our lives to awaken for the health and welfare of life in all its forms and manifestations. In this dedication, we must also include our care for the nature of the planet upon which we live, upon which we depend for our very existence. Increasingly meaningful is the welfare not only of sentient beings, but also of the living organism that is the planet itself, in all its beauty and diversity. We have an extraordinary gift in our human life of being able to recognise our own buddha-nature and how it can awaken, and also how we can bring awareness to the conservation and health of the planet upon which we live. Perhaps, in this, a bodhisattva has a new sense of meaningful engagement, which is to hold with compassion and wisdom the future of our very existence upon this planet.

10

Bodhicitta and Heart Essence

UP TO THIS POINT I have described the ingredients of what I have grown to feel constitute the essence of our potential experience of bodhicitta. In this I see bodhicitta as a *gestalt*, where the whole is greater than the sum of its parts. I have approached it in this way because I have always had the sense that we all have this potential within us but different aspects need help to emerge. As they do, our overall capacity to manifest this awakening heart or heart essence will also become more complete. A phrase in the bodhisattva vow says, "I will follow the training exactly as all bodhisattvas have done". We do not have to be perfect bodhisattvas right from the beginning. We practice and learn and gradually refine the qualities that make up the whole of what bodhicitta can be.

In this process we will begin to liberate a vitality within that brings with it an extraordinary gift. I recall many years ago Lama Zopa Rinpoche saying to me that with bodhicitta "just by touching someone you can heal them".

I found this remark very mysterious. To begin with I took this as an indication that opening the heart would heal others through the quality of compassionate holding and presence.

As my understanding of bodhicitta has deepened, however, I have seen another level of awakening this potential for healing. Bodhicitta, as the awakening heart essence, brings us into relationship with the very core of our buddha-nature as a healing source. This is not just a quality of intention or a quality of mind, it is also a quality of vitality or energy. Bodhicitta opens us to the source of our innate vitality also dwelling within the heart or, more specifically, within the heart chakra.

To begin to understand this process it may be helpful to approach it from a more tantric perspective regarding the nature of our body and our energetic nervous system. Our physical body is the vessel within which lives what is known in the tantric tradition as the subtle-body or energy-body. This energy-body is intimately connected to both our emotional life and our physical well-being and is the source in our life of vitality as well as potential discomfort and disturbance. It acts as a psychosomatic link that is not readily recognised in Western science but which has been understood for hundreds if not thousands of years in the East. On a deeper level, at the core or heart of the energy-body, is a quality of vitality that is essentially pure and extremely potent yet not necessarily consciously activated in our ordinary human condition. This vitality, when awakened, is the source of extraordinary qualities of love, joy, compassion and bliss and is particularly centred in the heart chakra. In the tantric tradition, this subtle vitality is sometimes called *tigle* in Tibetan or *bindu* in Sanskrit. It is also called bodhicitta and is a source of blissful wisdom energy that has great healing potential once awakened.

In the 1980s while living in India I spent a short time in Bodhgaya, where the Buddha attained enlightenment. While I was there I studied Shantideva's *Guide to the Bodhisattva's Way of Life* with a lama called Tara Tulku. He was the abbot of the local Tibetan monastery. He talked at length about the nature of bodhicitta as a quality of motivation, but I felt I was missing something. I went to visit him privately and asked the question: what does bodhicitta actually feel like? He was a very big man with a wonderful golden, round face and as he sat before me he leaned forward with a smile. I felt a sudden rush of extraordinary warm and blissful energy bursting in my heart and rushing through me. After what was probably only a minute he leaned back and the feeling stopped as though he had switched off a light. What Tara Tulku had shown me was a wonderful gift. I felt deeply touched by his heart essence of love and bliss. It was far from just a quality of intention to get enlightened for the sake of others.

This experience led me to consider that there was another side to bodhicitta that was very mysterious. While in retreat in India I had the opportunity to read some of Jung's collected works, and I was particularly interested in something he called the "treasure hard to attain"[17]. It was in reference to how, in the process of individuation, we would gradually discover a deep connection to a source of vitality that would awaken a capacity for health and wholeness. In his exploration of myths and fairy tales, he often saw the theme of a journey in search of a substance that would bring healing to the "kingdom". This kingdom he understood to be our sense of self that is in need of healing and restoration in order to become whole. The journey would entail passing through various trials that, once overcome, would lead eventually to finding this "treasure" that would restore the health of the kingdom. This healing source was often symbolised by objects such as a sacred spring, a fountain, an elixir, a sacred well or sacred pearl. Again, Jung saw in his study of mandalas in different cultures around the world that at the centre of a mandala there would almost always be a representation of this source, often in the form of a fountain, a well or a sacred object. In his exploration of the Middle Eastern alchemists, he also saw that this "treasure hard to attain" was an expression of the goal of alchemy. It was the philosopher's stone, lapis lazuli, the mercurial fountain or the elixir of life. The alchemists understood that the result of the process of transformation released the pure vitality at the core of our nature. It is interesting to note that, in *Guide to the Bodhisattva's Way of Life*, Shantideva also likens bodhicitta to a gold-making elixir that transforms our ordinary body into the body of a buddha.[18]

I read these ideas in Jung's collected works while I was in retreat, engaged in particular tantric practices that also referred to the source of vitality in our physical body as bodhicitta. I was fascinated by the similarity in the view from Jung's exploration and that within the tantric tradition. They both pointed to a pure vitality in our nature that was a source of extraordinary qualities of awakening as well as healing potential. As I have said, in the tantric tradition this is called *tigle* in Tibetan or *bindu* in Sanskrit. According to the tantric tradition, as we begin to awaken this vitality centred in our heart we touch into a quality that enables a much deeper, more subtle level of blissful wisdom energy. This subtle energy has the power to transform our ordinary nature into radiant "clear-light" wisdom energy imbued with the qualities of bliss, compassion and love.

Our awakening bodhicitta has many dimensions. There is the outer manifestation embodied in the world, engaged in ways that serve the welfare of others. There is the deep, feeling nature of bodhicitta imbued with qualities of love, compassion, joy and courage. There is the quality of awareness, known as ultimate bodhicitta, that is spacious and open, free of narrow, limiting, dualistic agendas. And there is also what might be seen as the secret level of bodhicitta, as an awakened potency of vitality that abides within the body and is centred in the heart chakra. This dimension is a more mystical aspect that is not often spoken of or taught, but which became very apparent to me in the extraordinary transmission from Tara Tulku that I described above. Within the tantric tradition we begin to understand this more esoteric sense of bodhicitta and see it as an opening to the *Source*. We begin to touch into a quality of vitality that will flow through us and become a source of love and joy as well as clarity and blissful wisdom. It will bring a greater capacity to engage in the world with a vitality that can accomplish what is needed in the service of others. It will also bring a very subtle capacity to sense into the suffering of others and, potentially, to heal.

As I have said earlier, it is bodhicitta that enables us to awaken to our innate buddha potential and live in the world as a bodhisattva. We discover the capacity to open to our innate wisdom nature and to the source of healing and transformation while remaining in the world to serve others. It bears repeating that this living between worlds is not easy and requires great courage and willingness to transform the challenges of life into a path of awakening.

But what else in life would give such a deep sense of
meaning?

11

The Bodhisattva

A BODHISATTVA IS ONE who embodies the quality of bodhicitta. As I said in an earlier chapter, the word bodhisattva is sometimes translated as the *awakening warrior*, implying the courage and willingness to remain embodied in the world of suffering in order to serve the welfare of others. As I began to describe in Chapter 5, a bodhisattva could be said to live between worlds or between two dimensions of reality. One dimension is the ultimate nature of reality: the primordial purity of spacious awareness, clarity and emptiness, free of dualistic appearances. The other is the dimension of relative truth and the world of forms and appearances within which we become entangled in our ordinary life. Living with full awareness of these two dimensions enables a profound capacity to remain in the world with all of its struggles and challenges while at the same time not be caught in holding them to be solid, enduring and truly existent. Put simply, this means the bodhisattva lives on the threshold between form and emptiness.

It is on this threshold that something extraordinary occurs, and to shed light on this I want to return to something I began to touch upon in Chapter 7. In our human condition we are endowed with three primary aspects to our nature: our mind, our energy-body and our physical body. These three are, from a tantric understanding, the basis of three potential attributes of the enlightened nature of a buddha, namely the three kayas.

The first of these aspects, our mind, is the basic ingredient that is refined and clarified into what then becomes a buddha's awakened mind. The mind's pure nature of clear, spacious, non-dual awareness has always been there within us but has been obscured by more gross and disturbed levels of mind. Once cleared of this veil of obscuration, it becomes the *wisdom truth body* or *dharmakaya* of a buddha.

The second aspect, our energy-body or subtle-body, is present within our gross physical body and is intimately connected to our emotional and feeling life. We could say that this energy-body is experienced within all the gross emotions and subtle nuances of our feeling life. For this reason, it is sometimes called the emotional body. The energy-winds (as this energy is often called) that are the underlying nature of our emotional life can be refined, healed and purified so that they become increasingly subtle and fluid. This brings them gradually into relationship with their underlying subtle "wisdom" energy that is also present within our physical body but is obscured by the more gross levels of movement and disturbance. Once refined and transformed, however, this energy-body becomes the basis of an extraordinary creative vitality that, in its awakened aspect, is known as the *sambhogakaya* or *enjoyment body* of a buddha.

The third aspect of our nature is the physical body, which is intimately connected to the energy-body which abides within it. The physical body reflects the relative state of health, sickness or discomfort of our constitution. In its present human condition this is often characterised by its pains and sicknesses on the one hand as well as its qualities and capabilities on the other. Because this physical body is the vehicle within which the other two "bodies" or kayas dwell, it is usually known as the *manifestation* or *emanation body*, the *nirmanakaya* of a buddha.

While the term kaya is most often used to refer to their presence in an awakened buddha, the kayas are also aspects of our buddha-nature. This buddha-nature is present within all of us as a primordially pure essence that is, as I said earlier, obscured or veiled from our awareness. Although we may not be aware of their pure nature, the *kayas* nevertheless constitute our manifestation in the world. There is an additional, paradoxical aspect to these three kayas. From one perspective we could say that they are simultaneously present in each moment; from another we can also recognise them as an unfolding process happening throughout our life.

The implication of these three kayas is that they are active and functional in our human condition right now, and we actually experience that functionality constantly in our day-to-day life. In the creative process, the mind is there on a relatively subtle level; it is the basic ground of awareness that may begin to germinate a thought or idea. I experience this, for example, in the many ways I express myself creatively. Though a thought or idea has not yet taken form, it begins to stir my imaginative faculty within my energetic nature, creating images or visions of what may be possible. These images or visions can activate an energetic intention that moves me towards some kind of expression. The energetic intention then begins to move through my body as an impulse to act, to do something or create something.

The notion that an idea "came out of the blue" is perhaps more significant than we think. Out of the subtle and formless nature of our mind – often symbolised in the tantric tradition by the colour blue – comes the movement of energy to begin to create. As this comes into the embodied process of creation, we complete the circuit. There is a natural movement, from dharmakaya through the energy of sambhogakaya into the embodied form of nirmanakaya (see Figure 4). This is a natural process in our daily life that a bodhisattva begins to embody more and more consciously. On the threshold between emptiness and form is an extraordinary dynamic of energy, or vitality. This natural impulse of the gradual movement from emptiness into expression and form is the enlivening, inspiring and igniting energy that moves us to be creative and expressive in our lives.

The bodhisattva within the tantric tradition cultivates the capacity to do a number of things in relation to these three kayas. First is the willingness to remain in the embodied form of nirmanakaya and maintain a quality of groundedness, balance and courage to stay engaged in the world even though times may be hard. We can see that, at this time in history, this is needed more than ever because the world is so full of collective fear and insecurity. We sorely need the steadiness of that grounded nature that does not become embroiled in the expressions of despair or anger and hatred.

Second, while clearly and steadily remaining in this embodied ground, a bodhisattva stays open to the subtle nature of the other two kayas. This connection to the "Source", the spacious clarity and pristine awareness of dharmakaya, provides a "ground of being" that is free of entanglement in the relative duality of our life. From this totally open clarity there is a natural flow of energy through sambhogakaya that nourishes and brings inspiration and vitality into the body. It is as though a bodhisattva, standing in this clear alignment of the three aspects of mind, energy and body, becomes a channel for something to come through from the most subtle level of our reality into embodied form. What is that something? Through this way of being, we can be a conduit for wisdom energy to come into expression in the world with love, compassion and creative inspiration that genuinely serves the welfare of others.

Third, for the tantric bodhisattva, the awakening of the energetic nature of sambhogakaya is enhanced by a relationship to a deity. The deity dwells in that intermediate ground between emptiness and form, bringing aspects of our buddha potential into manifestation as what Urgyen Tulku calls "spontaneous presence" [19]. Some of the deities that abide in this sambhogakaya ground are seen as expressions of particular bodhisattva qualities. Chenrezig is the expression of compassionate presence, Manjushri of wisdom communication, Vajrapani of the power to be effective and Green Tara as the dynamic expression of compassion. (The nature and quality of this particular group of deities will be found within many of the books within the *Essence of Tantra Series.* If you are interested to know more of their qualities and practice I would recommend reading these books.) As the capacity to embody these deity qualities deepens, a bodhisattva becomes increasingly able to manifest them into the world as an expression of bodhicitta to serve others in whatever way is the most beneficial.

At this time in history there is a crisis in our human condition. We are increasingly recognising the shadowy aspect of our nature and the reality of the world that this has created and continues to create. The devastation this shadow of ignorance can bring may feel overwhelming when we have no inner resource to tap into to give a sense of possibility and hope. Although our lives may be on the brink of major change upon this planet, we do not have to see this as a complete disaster. It is, on one level, a healing crisis. Amidst the dark time of this process a bodhisattva has a very significant role to play. Even though, as Lama Yeshe put it, we may only be "baby bodhisattvas", we can still contribute to this healing process if we know how.

When we stand in an alignment of the three kayas in our nature, we begin to become a conduit for what is clear, pure and radiant in our nature to come through. There is a natural flow between these three in both directions, from subtle through to form and back again. At this point these three kayas may not be in their pure aspect, but they are nevertheless active in our being. It is a bodhisattva's job to keep that channel open for the energy of the divine in our human nature to come into the world. Whether we call the source of this divinity dharmakaya or God, the difference may be just in the language. Whether we name that energy sambhogakaya or spirit, we are potentially opening to the same experience to come through. Our task as awakening bodhisattvas is to stay open to this connection and keep grounding it in the world like a lightning conductor. Our physical body is called the manifestation body or emanation body because this is what we need to begin to emanate. We emanate the love, wisdom, courage, openness and creative vitality into our reality. This can bring a sense of freshness and renewal at this time when, if our human race is to live upon this planet, things need to change and evolve in a healthy and positive way. Bodhicitta, the awakening of that energy of love, compassion and openness, is needed in the world today more than ever.

Figure 4

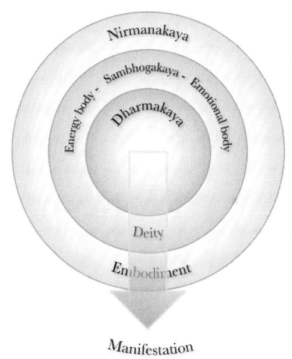

(This diagram is derived from one within the MA dissertation of Anna Murray Preece 2017)

1. A Tonglen Meditation

In the chapters on the four brahmaviharas I mentioned the practice of *tonglen* as a way of bringing together compassion and love within one meditation. There are many different approaches to tonglen; what I will describe here is one version that I have found most effective. I suggest beginning this meditation by bringing into the heart the presence of either Chenrezig or Green Tara.

*****

Begin by settling on the natural rising and falling of the breath. With an awareness of the quality of the out-breath, begin to settle into the body.

After a while, take part of your awareness down to the ground of the body and allow your entire body to rest and settle in that ground. (By ground I mean the sensation of the weight of the body on the cushion or chair and the sensation in the legs and pelvic floor.)

Bring your awareness gradually up into the body to become aware of sensation and feeling. Allow whatever is arising to be as it is without reaction or judgement, giving it space to move through.

Gradually become aware of the presence of either Chenrezig or Green Tara resting in your heart on a lotus and moon disc.

After a while bring into your awareness, in the space before you, someone you wish to do the tonglen practice in relation to. This could be an aspect of yourself as a child if there was some particular time when something happened that needs healing. You could choose one person or a few people, but to begin with not too many.

Begin to tune in to the pain, suffering, distress or difficulty of that person before you. Take your time to feel into this. Then think:

How wonderful it would be if this person could be free of suffering and the causes of suffering.
May they be free of suffering and its cause,
May I free them from suffering and its cause,
Bless me all you buddhas to be able to do this.

As you breathe in, begin to take in that suffering in the form of grey smoke. As you breathe that smoke in, it goes down to Chenrezig or Tara in your heart. When it touches the deity it is transformed into the light of compassion and absorbed.

Continue this in-breath for some time, getting a clearer sense of the person being gradually liberated from their suffering and feeling lighter and less burdened.

After some time, stop the breathing visualisation and feel into how that is for you.

Then begin to consider what might be beneficial to help this person and bring them a sense of satisfaction and happiness. Think:

How wonderful it would be if this person were endowed with happiness and the cause of happiness.
May they be endowed with happiness and its cause,
May I endow them with happiness and its cause,
Bless me all you buddhas to be able to do this.

As you breathe out, send a radiant light of love out from your heart and the deity in your heart. Think that this light fulfils what the person needs, to bring a feeling of satisfaction and happiness.

Have the sense that the person is changing and becoming more fulfilled and happy.

After some time, stop the breathing visualisation and rest with whatever feeling remains for you.

It is then helpful to spend a short while reciting the mantra of either Chenrezig or Tara, emanating healing light out to the person. This light blesses their body, speech and mind.

Finally, either bring that person into your heart and the heart of the deity, or allow them to return to their natural abode.

Conclude with a dedication.

2. An Equanimity Meditation

I have included the contemplation that follows as an example of how we might approach changing our response to someone who evokes strong reactions. Reflecting in this way can bring us back to a place of greater equanimity and balance in our view. It is important in this process to not deny or judge our own feelings, rather to be able to gradually let them move through to come to a less reactive awareness.

*****

Begin by settling on the natural rising and falling of the breath. With an awareness of the quality of the out-breath, begin to settle into the body.

Bring into the space before you someone you feel a strong negative reaction towards, whether anger, irritation, repulsion, hostility, jealousy or something else.

Spend some time feeling into the reactions you have, looking at your emotional response to this person. Stay with this for a while, allowing yourself to feel what you feel without judgement. Notice how those feelings orient around a "vivid" sense of I. What is that like? What is being "triggered"?

Recognise this and allow it freedom to begin to soften and move through. Try not to solidify and hold onto this response. Allow yourself to return to a quieter more regulated space of awareness.

Begin to look at what it is about them that you react to. Can you recognise what this leads you to project onto this person? Can you see how this might live in you as an aspect of your own nature? They may embody an aspect of your own shadow, an aspect of yourself that you feel is unacceptable.

Begin to consider the person behind your reaction projection. Try to recognise their struggles and suffering as well as their qualities, developing a more balanced view. Let that recognition enable a sense of kindness and compassion and understanding to grow. Remain with this for some time to let it settle in.

Think to yourself: because of my reaction projection I do not really see the suffering that goes on in their own life and experiences. I do not recognise the wounds and problems that are potentially there at the root of their experience. I do not readily see their qualities and abilities.

Stay with the result of this reflection and sense into whether your view of this person is changing. Allow a sense of compassion and equanimity to grow.

Remain with the felt experience that is left.

Apramana	Skt. Infinite mind. Term used for the four immeasurables.
Arhant	Skt. One who has become liberated from the cycle of existence.
Bindu	Skt. Elemental fluid drops in the body, Tib. Tigle. Also called bodhicitta.
Bodhicitta	Skt. The awakening mind or heart essence; the intention to awaken for the welfare of sentient beings.
Bodhisattva	Skt. One who is engaged in the path to awaken for the welfare of sentient beings. The awakening warrior.
Brahmavihara	Skt. Literally: The abode of Brahma, known as the four immeasurables.
Chakra	Skt. Literally: Wheel – conjunction of channels in the central channel of the energy-body.
Chenrezig	Tib. The buddha of compassion. Skt. Avalokiteshvara.

Dharma	Skt. Literally: Truth or true; the Buddha's teachings.
Dharmakaya	Skt. The wisdom or "truth body" of a buddha.
Dzogchen	Tib. Literally: Great completion; meditation on the natural clarity of the mind.
Guru	Tib. Lama; teacher.
Individuation	Jungian term. The process of self-actualisation (not individualism).
Kaya	Skt. Literally: Body. As in a body of water.
Kum nye	Tib. System of physical healing exercises introduced by Tarthang Tulku.
Lam rim	Tib. Graduated path.
Mahakala	Skt. A fierce Dharma protector; a wrathful manifestation of Chenrezig.
Mahamudra	Skt. Meditation on the mind's innate clarity and awareness.
Mahayana	Skt. Literally: The great vehicle; sometimes called the northern school of Buddhism, found today in Tibet, China and Japan.
Mandala	Skt. A circular configuration with a central axis.
Ngöndro	Tib. Preliminary practices.
Nirmanakaya	Skt. The emanation or manifestation body of a buddha.

Numinous	Jungian term: A highly charged experience of awe and fascination.
Rinpoche	Tib. Literally: Precious; the name given to a reincarnated lama.
Sambhogakaya	Skt. The "enjoyment body" or purified energy-body of a buddha.
Self	Jungian term: The centre of our totality. Archetypal root of meaning.
Shantideva	Skt. A highly revered 11th-century Indian scholar.
Tara	Skt. A female tantric meditation deity, the embodiment of active compassion and all accomplishing wisdom.
Tigle	Tib. Elemental fluid drops in the body. Skt. Bindu.
Tonglen	Tib. Literally: Giving and taking. A meditation practice for the cultivation of compassion and love.
Tulku	Tib. A reincarnated lama, usually called Rinpoche. Skt. Nirmanakaya.
Tantra	Skt. The Buddha's esoteric teaching.

[1] Just as a flash of lightning on a dark cloudy night
For an instant brightly illuminates all
Likewise in this world, through the might of the buddhas,
A wholesome thought rarely and briefly appears.
Shantideva, Guide to the Bodhisattva's Way of Life, ch. 1 v.4.
[2] Universal Responsibility and the Good Heart. H.H.
Dalai Lama.
[3] Herbert Guenther, *Kindly Bent to Ease Us,* Longchenpa,
ch. 7, Page 108.
[4] Shantideva, *Guide to the Bodhisattva's Way of Life*, ch. 7,
Enthusiasm.
[5] Tarthang Tulku. *The Joy of Being.* Instruction on the
practice of Kum Nye.
[6] Six causes and one effect, meditation instruction found
within the teachings of the lam rim, or graduated path,
on the cultivation of bodhicitta. See *The Essential Nectar,*
Geshe Rabten, Meditation 9.
[7] Shantideva, *Guide to the Bodhisattva's Way of Life*,
ch. 7, Enthusiasm, v. 46-49.
[8] Shantideva, *Guide to the Bodhisattva's Way of Life*,
ch. 4, Conscientiousness, v.1-8.

[9] Bodhisattva vow:

All you buddhas and bodhisattvas please listen to what I now say from the depth of my heart,

Just as the buddhas of the past have developed the thought of enlightenment, true bodhicitta,

Then practiced its stages of graded development, following the trainings of all Buddha's sons and daughters,

So may I too, for the sake of all beings, develop bodhicitta and follow the training exactly as all bodhisattvas have done.

[10] The 2nd-century Indian scholar/saint Nāgārjuna is widely considered to be the founder of the Madhyamaka school of Buddhist philosophy. His *Mulamadhyamakakarika* is perhaps the most important text on the Madhyamaka philosophy of emptiness.

[11] From *The Ego and the Dynamic Ground* by Michael Washburn, ch. 4.

[12] Heruka sadhana by Pabonka Rinpoche, translated by Rob Preece.

[13] Mandala offering in *Preparing for Tantra,* by Rob Preece, ch. 13.

[14] *Mandala and Visions of Wholeness,* by RobPreece

[15] *Man and His Symbols,* edited by C.G. Jung.

[16] For the mandala of a deity see: *Mandala and Visions of Wholeness* by Rob Preece.

[17] *Symbols of Transformation,* C.G. Jung. Collected works Vol. 5 pp. 71, 118.

[18] Shantideva's "gold-making elixir", *Guide to the Bodhisattva's Way of Life,* ch. 1, v.10.

[19] Spontaneous presence is the term Urgyen Tulku uses to refer to the natural capacity of pure awareness to spontaneously manifest in form as a compassionate display of emptiness for the welfare of sentient beings. From *As it is* by Urgyen Tulku.

Bibliography

Arya Maitreya and Asanga. *The Changeless Nature: The Mahayana Uttara Tantra Shastra.* Trans. Ken and Katia Holmes. Eskdalemuir: Kagyu Samye Ling, 1985.

Dalai Lama. *Beyond Religion, Ethics for a Whole World.* London: Rider, 2012.

Dalai Lama. *Essence of the Heart Sutra.* Trans. and ed. Thupten Jinpa. Boston: Wisdom Publications, 2005.

Dalai Lama. *Stages of Meditation.* Ithaca: Snow Lion Publications, 2001.

Dalai Lama & Alexander Berzin. *The Gelug/Kagyu Tradition of Mahamudra.* Ithaca: Snow Lion Publications, 1997.

Dhargyey, Geshe Ngawang. *The Tibetan Tradition of Mental Development.* Dharamsala: Library of Tibetan Works and Archives, 1974.

Dzogchen Ponlop. *Wild Awakening; The Heart of Mahamudra and Dzogchen.* Boston: Shambhala Publications, 2003.

Edinger, Edward F. *Ego and Archetype.* Boston: Shambhala Publications, 1992.

Jacobi, Jolande. *Complex/Archetype/Symbol in the Psychology of C. G. Jung.* Trans. Ralph Mannheim. Princeton: Princeton University Press/Bollingen Foundation, 1971.

Jung, C.G. *Alchemical Studies*. Ed. and trans. Gerhard Adler and R. F. C. Hull. The Collected Works of C. G. Jung. Vol. 13. Princeton: Princeton University Press/Bollingen Foundation, 1983.

Jung, C.G. *Archetypes and the Collective Unconscious*. Ed. and trans. Gerhard Adler and R.F.C. Hull. The Collected Works of C. G. Jung. Vol. 9, Part 1. Princeton: Princeton University Press/Bollingen Foundation, 1981.

Jung, C.G., ed. *Man and His Symbols*. New York: Anchor Books, Doubleday, 1964.

Jung, C.G. *Psychology and Alchemy*. Ed. and trans. Gerhard Adler and R. F. C. Hull. The Collected Works of C. G. Jung. Vol. 12. Princeton: Princeton University Press/Bollingen Foundation, 1980.

Jung,C.G. *Psychology and Religion: West and East*. Ed. and trans. Gerhard Adler and R.F. C. Hull. The Collected Works of C. G. Jung. Vol. 11. Princeton: Princeton University Press/Bollingen Foundation, 1970.

Khenchen Thrangu Rinpoche. *Essentials of Mahamudra*. Boston: Wisdom, 2004.

Khenchen Thrangu Rinpoche. *An Ocean of the Ultimate Meaning: Teachings on Mahamudra*. Boston: Shambhala Publications, 2004.

Levine, Peter A. *Waking the Tiger*. Berkeley: North Atlantic Books, 1997.

Long Chen Pa. *Kindly Bent to Ease Us. Part One: Mind*. Trans. and annot. Herbert V Guenther. Emeryville: Dharma Publishing, 1975.

Long Chen Rab Jampa, H.H Dudjom Rinpoche, Beru Khyentze Rinpoche. *The Four Themed Precious Garland*. Dharamsala: Library of Tibetan Works and Archives, 1979.

Phabongka Rinpoche. *Commentary on the Heruka Body Mandala* (in Tibetan). Unpublished translation.

Phabongka Rinpoche. *The Sadhana of Chakrasamvara* (in Tibetan). Unpublished translation.

Preece, Rob. *The Courage to Feel.* Ithaca: Snow Lion Publications, 2009.

Preece, Rob. *Preparing for Tantra: Creating the Psychological Ground for Practice.* Ithaca: Snow Lion Publications, 2011.

Preece, Rob. *The Psychology of Buddhist Tantra.* Ithaca: Snow Lion Publications, 2006.

Preece, Rob. *Tasting the Essence of Tantra: Buddhist Meditation for Contemporary Western Life.* Devon: Mudra Publications, 2018.

Preece, Rob. *The Wisdom of Imperfection.* Ithaca: Snow Lion Publications, 2006.

Rabten, Geshe. *The Essential Nectar: Meditations on the Buddhist Path.* Boston: Wisdom Publications, 1984.

Rabten, Geshe. *The Preliminary Practices of Tibetan Buddhism.* Dharamsala: Library of Tibetan Works and Archives, 1974.

Rabten, Geshe and Geshe Ngawang Dhargyey. *Advice from a Spiritual Friend: Tibetan Teachings on Buddhist Thought Transformation.* New Delhi: Publications for Wisdom Culture, 1977.

Rosenberg, Larry, with David Guy. *Breath by Breath: The Liberating Practice of Insight Meditation.* Boston: Shambhala, 2004.

Shantideva: *Guide to the Bodhisattva's way of life.* Trans. Stephen Bachelor. Dharamsala: Library of Tibetan Works and Archives,1979.

Sonam Rinchen, Geshe. *The Three Principle Aspects of the Path.* Ithaca: Snow Lion Publications, 1999.

Tarthang Tulku. *Gesture of Balance.* Berkeley: Dharma

Publishing, 1977.

Tarthang Tulku. *The Joy of Being.* California: Dharma Publishing, 2006.

Tarthang Tulku. *Kum Nye Relaxation, Part 2: Relaxation Exercises.* Berkeley: Dharma Publishing, 1978.

Tsongkhapa. *Three Principal Aspects of the Path.* Trans. Alexander Berzin. Dharamsala: Library of Tibetan Works and Archives, 1982.

Washburn, Michael. *The Ego and the Dynamic Ground: A Transpersonal Theory of Human Development.* Albany: State University of New York Press, 1995.

Yeshe, Lama Thubten. *Becoming the Compassion Buddha.* Boston: Wisdom Publications, 2003.

Yeshe, Lama Thubten. *Mahamudra.* Boston: Wisdom Publications, 1981.

About the Author

Following an apprenticeship in electronics engineering Rob Preece went to university to study psychology. It was at this time he met both the work of C.G. Jung and Buddhism. After university, a period of travel led him to Nepal where, in 1973, he met his teachers Lama Thubten Yeshe and Lama Zopa Rinpoche.

Rob was a social worker for 3 years and then, in 1976, he was part of a small group that founded a Buddhist centre in the UK for his Tibetan teachers. For the next four years he studied the foundations of Tibetan practice in that Buddhist community. In 1980 he returned to India and was in retreat for much of the next five years. This gave him a chance to explore the practices of the tantric tradition in some depth, meditating under the guidance of Lama Yeshe, Zopa Rinpoche and Gen Jhampa Wangdu in particular. While in India he was fortunate enough to receive teachings and tantric empowerments from lamas such as H.H. Dalai Lama, Song Rinpoche, Lati Rinpoche and many others. It also gave him the opportunity to learn thangka (tantric icon) painting. Rob has also received dzogchen teachings from H.H. Dudjom Rinpoche, then head of the Nyingma tradition, and more recently from Tsok Nyi Rinpoche.

After returning to the West Rob trained as a psychotherapist with the Centre for Transpersonal Psychology in London. This began the process of bringing together the two worlds of Buddhism and Jungian psychology as a practicing psychotherapist. Since 1985 he has been leading meditation retreats following the guidance of his teachers. Lama Yeshe was particularly influential in this, supporting his integration of a more Western approach. Rob's one-to-one work is now principally spiritual mentoring, bringing together his experience of both Eastern and Western approaches.

Rob leads meditation retreats in the UK, Europe and the US. In the UK, some of these retreats incorporate a movement practice facilitated by his wife Anna. As a father of two sons, an experienced thangka painter and a keen gardener he tries to ground Buddhist practice in a creative practical lifestyle. He is the author of many books bridging the Tibetan tradition with Western psychology, intended to support Buddhist practice in contemporary life. These include: *The Psychology of Buddhist Tantra*; *The Wisdom of Imperfection*; *The Courage to Feel*; *Preparing for Tantra*; *Feeling Wisdom* and *Tasting the Essence of Tantra*.

Essence of Tantra Series

In this new series of books following his *Tasting the Essence of Tantra,* Rob takes specific areas of tantra into more depth. He continues to follow the principles first taught by his teacher Lama Thubten Yeshe, bringing together the worlds of Western psychology and Buddhist understanding. It is his unique depth of experience of both worlds that gives this series its aliveness and creativity. New and experienced practitioners alike will find these books invaluable in deepening the effectiveness of the tantric path.

The series will contain the following books:

The Mandala and Visions of Wholeness: Within Tibetan Buddhism and Jungian Psychology

Heart Essence: Enhancing Qualities of the Awakening Mind

Manjushri: The Creative Expression of Wisdom

Chenrezig: Embodying Compassionate Presence

Vajrapani: Clarifying our Relationship to Power

Green Tara: Embodying Dynamic Compassion

**For information relating to these books and Rob's work, go to
www.mudra.co.uk
If you have enjoyed this book, please feel free to put a review on Amazon.**

Made in the USA
Columbia, SC
07 June 2024